KW-484-857

Local Government
and the
Elected Member

AN ROINN COMHSHAOIL, OIDHREACHTA AGUS RIALTAIS ÁITIÚIL

DEPARTMENT OF THE ENVIRONMENT, HERITAGE
AND LOCAL GOVERNMENT

© Department of the Environment, Heritage
and Local Government 2004

Baile Átha Cliath
Arna Fhoilsiú ag Oifig an tSoláthair

Le ceannach díreach ón
Oifig Dhíolta Foilseachán Rialtais
Teach Sun Alliance
Sráid Theach Laighean, Baile Átha Cliath 2

nó tríd an bpost ó
Foilseacháin Rialtais, An Rannóg Po.**'-Tráchta**
51 Faiche Stiabhna, Baile Átha Clia\.**'1 2**
(Teil: 01 - 6476834/35/36/37; Fax: 01 - 64/.**5843)**
nó trí aon díoltóir leabhar.

Dublin
Published by the Stationery Office

To be purchased directly from the
Government Publications Sale Office
Sun Alliance House
Molesworth Street, Dublin 2

or by mail order from
Government Publications, Postal Trade Section
51 St. Stephen's Green, Dublin 2
(Tel: 01 - 6476834/35/36/37; Fax: 01 - 6476843)
or through any bookseller.

€5

ISBN 0-7557-1934-4

Designed by Butler Claffey Design, Dublin
Typeset by Typeform Repro, Dublin
Printed in Ireland by Future Print, Dublin

Local Government
and the
Elected Member

AN ROINN COMHSHAOIL, OIDHREACHTA AGUS RIALTAIS ÁITIÚIL

DEPARTMENT OF THE ENVIRONMENT, HERITAGE
AND LOCAL GOVERNMENT

Contents

Foreword

This booklet has been supplied to all local authorities for distribution to incoming councillors following the local elections this month. It provides an outline of the local government system and the role and powers vested in the elected members. At a time of change it is my hope that it will help councillors to carry out their role as the formulators of local authority policy, in working with the executive for the common good and to maintain an overview and give general direction to local authority affairs. This is a demanding remit. As with other public agencies, the public quite rightly expect local authorities – the public representatives whom they elect and the officials alike – to operate at all times in a professional manner and to very high standards. Local government has served the community well over the years and I have no doubt it will continue to meet the demanding challenges that lie ahead. To this end, I wish each councillor every success during their coming term of office.

Martin Cullen T.D.
Minister for the Environment, Heritage and Local Government
June 2004

Réamhrá

 Tá an leabhrán seo á chur ar fáil do gach údarás áitiúil le dáileadh ar chomhairleoirí nua i ndiaidh na dtoghchán áitiúil an mhí seo. Tugann sé léargas ar an gcóras rialtais áitiúil agus ar an ról agus ar na cumhachtaí atá dílsithe do na baill tofa. Sa tráth athraitheach seo, tá súil agam go gcabhróidh sé le comhairleoirí agus iad ag cruthú polasaí dá n-údarás áitiúil, agus ag obair leis an lucht feidhmiúcháin ar mhaithe leis an leas coiteann agus ag coinneáil súil leathan agus treoir ghinearálta ar chúrsaí údaráis áitiúil. Is sainchúram dúshlánach é seo, agus faoi mar atá i gcás áisíneachtaí poiblí eile, bíonn an pobal ag súil, agus an ceart acu, go bhfeidhmeoidh na húdaráis áitiúla – idir ionadaithe tofa agus oifigigh araon – i gcónaí ar bhonn gairmiúil agus de réir na gcaighdéan is airde.

Tá seirbhís an-mhaith tugtha ag an rialtas áitiúil don pobal thar na blianta agus níl aon amhras orm ach go leanfaidh sé leis ag riar ar na riachtanais dhúshlánacha a bheidh roimhe sna blianta amach anseo. Dá bhrí sin, is mian liom gach rath a ghuí ar na comhairleoirí go léir i rith a dtéarma nua in oifig.

Máirtín Ó Cuillinn T.D.
An tAire Comhshaoil, Oidhreachta agus Rialtais Áitiúil
Meitheamh 2004

Introduction

A booklet summarising the powers vested in the elected members of local authorities was first published by the then Department of Local Government in October 1955. This sixth edition of the booklet has been greatly expanded. It includes an overview of the local government system and sets out the role and powers of the elected council along with information on meetings, conduct of business, ethics and other matters of practical relevance to members. It takes account of developments, including new legislation, in the period of over a decade since the booklet was last revised and is based on the law applying as of early 2004.

It must be borne in mind however that a guide such as this does not present a complete statement of the law nor is it intended to. Likewise, it is not an authoritative or legal interpretation which ultimately in case of dispute may fall to the courts. Rather the aim is to provide a general overview and it is hoped that members of local authorities, particularly new members, will find the updated guide to be both informative and useful.

The Department wishes to acknowledge the input and assistance of the Institute of Public Administration in the preparation and publication of this booklet.

Department of the Environment, Heritage and Local Government
June, 2004

Local Authority Areas

Northern Ireland
District Council Boundary ———

A Carrickferg
B Newtownal
C Belfast
D Castlereag
E North Dow
F Ards

Buncrana
Coleraine
Moyle
Letterkenny
Limavady
Ballymoney
Derry
Ballymena
Larne
Donegal
Strabane
Magherafelt
Antrim
B
Cookstown
A
Omagh
C
D
Craigavon
Lisburn
E
F
Ballyshannon
Dungannon
Bundoran
Monaghan
Armagh
Banbridge
Down
Fermanagh
Monaghan
Sligo
Clones
Newry
Sligo
Belturbet
Castle-
and Mourne
Ballina
Cootehill
Ballybay
blayney
Dundalk
Leitrim
Cavan
Carrick-
Boyle
macross
Mayo
Louth
Castlebar
Ardee
Roscommon
Cavan
Westport
Granard
Drogheda
Longford
Kells
Balbriggan
Tuam
Longford
Navan
Westmeath
Trim
1
Galway
Athlone
Mullingar
Meath
Ballinasloe
Leixlip
Dublin
1 Fingal
Galway
Edenderry
2 South Dublin
Loughrea
Tullamore
Naas
2
3
3 Dun Laoghaire/
Offaly
Droichead Nua
Rathdown
Birr
Mountmellick
Bray
Clare
Portlaoise
Kildare
Greystones
Nenagh
Laois
Athy
Wicklow
Ennis
North
Templemore
Wicklow
Kilkee
Shannon
Tipperary
Thurles
Kilkenny
Carlow
Arklow
Kilrush
Limerick
Muinebheag
Gorey
Carlow
Kilkenny
Enniscorthy
Limerick
Tipperary
Cashel
Wexford
Listowel
South
Clonmel
Carrick
New Ross
Tipperary
on Suir
Wexford
Tralee
Waterford
Kerry
Fermoy
Waterford
Mallow
Lismore
Tramore
Killarney
Cork
Dungarvan
Midleton
Youghal
Macroom
Cobh
Cork
Passage West
Bandon
Kinsale
Bantry
Clonakilty
Skibbereen

County Boundary ———
City Councils ■
Borough Councils ●
Town Councils ●

Based on Ordnance Survey Ireland Permit No. 7835
© Ordnance Survey Ireland and Government of Ireland
and Ordnance Survey of Northern Ireland Permit No. 40182
© Crown Copyright 2004

Chapter 1

Local Government: An Overview

Section 1.1
Local Government Structures

Local Democracy

1.1.1 Local government plays a very significant part in the life of the nation. It is an integral part of the democratic process. Furthermore, the activities of local authorities have an important economic and social impact. Because of the role local authorities play, the range of matters for which they are responsible and their closeness to local communities, local government has a more immediate effect on the day-to-day lives of the people than most other sectors of public administration. But local government is different from other public sector agencies. It is democratically elected. Apart from Dáil Éireann and the Presidency, it is the only other institution whose members are directly elected by all of the people. Local government has therefore both a representational and an operational role, with responsibility for a range of services. It operates through a network of directly elected local authorities which provide, among other things, a forum for the democratic representation of local communities, giving expression to local identity, identifying local concerns and setting local priorities.

> *But local government is different from other public sector agencies. It is democratically elected. Apart from Dáil Éireann and the Presidency, it is the only other institution whose members are directly elected by all of the people.*

Local Government and the Legal Framework

1.1.2   Article 28A of the Constitution, which was approved by referendum in 1999, endorses the democratic representative role of local government and guarantees local elections at least every five years. It recognises the role of local government in exercising functions conferred by law and in promoting by its initiative local community interests. The Local Government Act 2001 is the basic legislation governing local government in Ireland today – structures, operations and functions. It consolidated much previous local government legislation into one text (some of it dating back to the Local Government (Ireland) Act 1898 and before) and provides the framework for the local government system. The Act provides that each local authority has an elected council with a Cathaoirleach and Leas-Chathaoirleach. It provides for the holding of local elections every five years and sets out a general statement of local government functions including its representational role and its role in the promotion of the interests of local communities. It should be noted however that, in addition to the 2001 Act, the operation of local authorities is affected by a whole range of other legislation, very often dealing with specific services (e.g. housing, roads, planning, waste etc) which should be consulted where relevant.

County Councils and City Councils

1.1.3   In local government terms, Ireland is divided into thirty-four areas – twenty-nine county council areas and five city council areas. These areas cover the entire State. The twenty-six historical counties which make up the State translate into twenty-nine local government counties. This is because County

Tipperary has traditionally had two local government counties, now called North Tipperary and South Tipperary; in addition since 1994 County Dublin has three local government counties, Fingal, South Dublin and Dún Laoghaire-Rathdown. The five cities are Cork, Dublin, Galway, Limerick and Waterford. Each operates as an independent and autonomous local authority and is entirely separate from its home county. Each of these thirty-four areas (the twenty-nine counties and five cities) has its own local authority elected by the local population and known as the county council or the city council, as appropriate.

Town Councils and Borough Councils

1.1.4   Within most county council areas (but not all), and forming part of them, are other local government areas known as towns. There are eighty such local government towns, each of which elects its own local authority known as a town council. In five of the eighty towns (Clonmel, Drogheda, Kilkenny, Sligo and Wexford) the title borough council is used. About 14 per cent of the total national population reside within the eighty local government towns, somewhat higher if environs are included. The residents of these towns vote in two separate elections held simultaneously – one for the town council and one for the county council. The residents of such towns are therefore represented by councillors elected both at town level and at county level – and indeed a number of councillors may be members of both authorities.

Change of Names

1.1.5   The Local Government Act 2001 updated older local government terminology and so references to former local

3

authority titles are still to be found in various pieces of legislation, reports etc. published before end 2001. The following table outlines the current local authority titles, along with the former ones which applied prior to 1 January 2002.

Title	Title Before 2002
County Council	No change with the exception of North Tipperary County Council and South Tipperary County Council, formerly known as Tipperary North Riding County Council and Tipperary South Riding County Council
City Council	County Borough Corporation
Borough Council	Borough Corporation
Town Council	Urban District Council or Town Commissioners

All the town-based local authorities (formerly known as borough corporations (5), urban district councils (49) and town commissioners (26)) are now known as town councils or borough councils. City councils were formerly known as county borough corporations.

1.1.6 All local authority members are now known as councillors replacing older terminology such as aldermen and commissioners which no longer apply. Likewise under the 2001 Act the chairperson and vice-chairperson are known as the Cathaoirleach or Leas-Chathaoirleach but with flexibility for different titles to apply (see 2.3.3).

Section 1.2
Local Government Functions

1.2.1   Local authorities are multi-purpose bodies responsible for an extensive range of services. The annual budget of local authorities is formulated under eight main programme groups. An outline of local authority activities/services presented in this general format is listed in the table on page 6. Although the list does not exhaust the range of local authority activity, it gives a useful indication of the overall spread. Moreover, in a broader context, local authorities are concerned with the promotion of the general economic, social and cultural development of their areas and work with other agencies and interests to promote progress. (See also county/city development boards at 6.1.)

1.2.2   The full range of local authority functions as set out in the table on page 6 rests with the county and city councils, as the primary units of local government. In the case of some functions (e.g. library, motor tax, water services and usually national roads and fire services) the county council has responsibility throughout the entire county including the towns. Town councils exercise functions to varying degrees within the towns concerned, from a fairly extensive role for some to a mainly representational role in case of certain town councils. However all local authorities exercise a representational role and enjoy broad powers to support the community interest, to make bye-laws to regulate local matters and may raise a community contribution to support local projects. Town councils are also represented on the relevant county council area committee (see 2.5.5). The Local Government Act 2001 requires that county councils and town councils work together to provide a unified service to the public.

Programme Group	Summary of activities/ services
Housing and building	Provision of social housing, assessment of housing needs, housing strategies, homelessness, housing loans and grants, Traveller accommodation, voluntary housing, private rented sector and housing standards
Roads and transportation	Road construction and maintenance, traffic management, public lighting, collection of motor taxes, driver licences, taxi licensing
Water and sewerage Planning and development	Water supply, waste water treatment, group water schemes, public conveniences Adoption of development plan, decisions on planning applications, urban or village renewal plans and works, heritage protection, industrial and tourism infrastructure and support
Environmental protection	Waste collection and disposal, waste management planning, litter prevention, the fire service, civil defence, air/water pollution controls, burial grounds, building safety
Recreation and amenity	Public libraries, parks and open spaces, swimming pools, recreation centres, the arts, culture, museums, galleries and other amenities
Agriculture, education, health and welfare Miscellaneous services	Making nominations to vocational education committees and harbour boards, processing of higher education grants, veterinary services Maintaining the register of electors for elections, financial management, rate collection, provision of animal pounds

The summary of the programme groups has been adjusted somewhat for presentational purposes.

1.2.3   Apart from the specific statutory functions of local authorities, councillors represent their electorate over a range of public issues and would thus have a concern with, for example, the operation of other public agencies within their area and its general development. Local authorities also have a right of representation on a range of other public agencies which operate locally, such as vocational education committees, harbour boards and LEADER groups. Additionally, with the advent of county/city development boards, local government now has a direct role in promoting the co-ordination of various public agencies operating locally (See 6.1).

1.2.4   Faoin Acht um Rialtas Áitiúil 2001, tá ról ag na húdaráis áitiúla chun úsáid na Gaeilge a chur chun cinn. Chuige sin, is féidir cruinnithe a bheith acu i nGaeilge nó i mBéarla nó sa dá theanga. Forálann an tAcht céanna orthu grúpa comhairleach a bhunú i dtaobh úsáid na teanga ag údaráis áitiúla. Tá na forálacha seo neartaithe ag Acht na dTeangacha Oifigiúla 2003. Tá tacaíocht sheasmhach tugtha ag an gcóras rialtais áitiúil chun an Ghaeilge a chur chun cinn. An dea-thoil atá ann don teanga i measc na mball tofa agus i measc fhoireann na n-údarás áitiúil, is cuid fíorthábhachtach é den tacaíocht agus den chur chun cinn seo. Ar leibhéal praiticiúil, tá go leor de na húdaráis áitiúla i bhfíorthosach chun an Ghaeilge a chur cinn agus cruinnithe á reachtáil ó am go ham i nGaeilge nó i mBéarla agus Gaeilge, a thugann deis agus spreagadh do gach duine páirt a ghlacadh ag a leibhéal féin.

Section 1.3

Local Government Finance

1.3.1   The impact of local government on the social and economic life of the country both as providers of service and purchasers of goods and services is very substantial. For example in 2003 local authorities spent over €7 billion, about half of which consisted of current expenditure and half of capital expenditure. Capital and current expenditure are funded in different ways.

Capital Expenditure

1.3.2   Capital expenditure differs significantly from current expenditure in that it is expenditure that results in the creation of an asset beyond the year in which that asset is originally provided. Examples would include construction of local authority houses, road construction, provision of water and sewerage facilities, library and swimming pool facilities. Capital expenditure is financed largely by State grants (in future some grants may be replaced by Public Private Partnership (PPP) funding) with the balance being funded from borrowings and by local authorities' own internal resources such as development levies and property sales. In the case of some projects (e.g. local authority offices) they may be funded entirely by local authority own resources and borrowing.

Current Expenditure

1.3.3   The local authority's annual budget is based on current expenditure (sometimes referred to as revenue expenditure) which covers the day-to-day running of the local authority (including staff salaries, housing maintenance, pensions, operational costs of treatment plants etc.). The annual budget is adopted by the elected council at its budget meeting. For further information on the budgetary process and the control exercised by the council see 4.4. Current expenditure is funded from a variety of sources, as set out below, although the specific distribution of income from the different sources may vary between authorities.

Sources of Income for Current Expenditure 2003

Rates	24%
Charges for Goods and Services	33%
Specific State Grants	25%
Local Government Fund - general purpose grant	18%
Total	100%

Rates, as well as charges for goods and services, are local sources of income over which local authorities have a considerable measure of control, while specific and general purpose grants are paid annually to local authorities by the State.

1.3.4   Rates are levied annually by county, city, borough and certain town councils. Each of these authorities has exclusive rating jurisdiction within its own area. Some town councils are not themselves rating authorities and there may be an additional charge to the county rate levied on such towns to meet the expenses of the town council. As a general rule, rates are levied on the occupiers of commercial property. The valuation of such property for rating purposes is carried out by a central government agency, the Valuation Office, with a right of appeal to a Valuation Tribunal. Each year the level of the rate (known as the Annual Rate on Valuation or ARV) is determined by the elected council as part of the budgetary process. The annual rates bill for a commercial premises is calculated by applying this rate to the valuation of the property concerned.

1.3.5 Local authorities have powers to charge for services which they provide, for example, commercial water charges, housing rents, waste charges, parking charges, planning application fees. In most cases the charge or fee is set locally although certain charges or fees are fixed at national level.

1.3.6 The Local Government Fund (LGF) is a special central fund into which is lodged the full proceeds of motor tax receipts along with a contribution from the national Exchequer. Local authorities are then allocated general purpose grants annually from the Fund to assist in the financing of their current expenditure. These grants are block grants and can be used by authorities at their discretion. The Fund is also the source for non-national road grants which must be used for that purpose. Specific State grants are also made to local authorities. These embrace different aspects of their operations and are paid by a number of government departments. Such grants generally provide for expenditure incurred by local authorities in respect of specific services/schemes, for example higher education grants, road maintenance grants etc.

Section 1.4
Elected Members, Management and Staff

1.4.1 Under the Local Government Act 2001 each local authority (city council, county council, borough council and town council) has an elected council with members known as councillors who are elected every five years. The Act sets out the number of members for each local authority.

1.4.2 The elected council is the policy-making arm of the local authority, who act by what are termed 'reserved functions'. Reserved functions are defined by law and specified across a whole range of enactments. These comprise mainly decisions on important matters of policy and finance (e.g. adoption of annual budget, development plan, bye-laws). The day-to-day management of the local authority, including staffing matters, is vested in a full time chief executive – known as the county or city manager. The manager and/or staff to whom functions are delegated discharge what are termed 'executive functions' – in effect these involve the day-to-day running of the authority within the policy parameters as determined by the council. Any function of a local authority that is not specified in law as a reserved function is deemed to be an executive function. The legal character of a local authority thus comprises two elements, the elected council of the authority and the manager, with responsibility for performing local authority functions shared between them. However, legally all functions, whether performed by the elected council or by the county/city manager, are exercised on behalf of the local authority.

1.4.3 While the law must make a precise division of functions so that responsibility for their exercise may be clearly defined, in practice the policy and executive roles are intended to be complementary. The council and manager operate together, with the former having the pre-eminent role through the determination of the policy framework and with arrangements to maintain an overview of local authority affairs generally. A fuller description of the system is set out in Chapter 4.

South Dublin Headquarters, Concourse Area

Chapter 2

Local Authorities: Membership and Conduct of Business

Section 2.1
Membership of Local Authorities

2.1.1 The number of members of each local authority is fixed by law and the members are known as county, city, borough or town councillors as appropriate. The elected council of a local authority comprises the councillors elected or co-opted to that authority. Any person eighteen years or over who is a citizen of Ireland or is ordinarily resident in the State is eligible to become a member of a local authority, subject to certain disqualifications. Among those disqualified are specified EU office holders; MEPs; Oireachtas members; Gardaí; members of the Defence Forces; certain civil servants and local authority staff; persons convicted of certain offences. The Constitution stipulates that local elections must be held at least every five years.

2.1.2 A person may nominate himself/herself as a candidate for election or, with his/her consent, may be nominated by a local government elector registered in the local electoral area (LEA) of the authority for which it is proposed to nominate the candidate. A person can be nominated to stand in more than one LEA. A candidate from a registered political party must attach a certificate of political affiliation to the nomination form; in the case of non-party candidates the form must have the assent of fifteen persons registered in the LEA concerned.

2.1.3 Persons eighteen years of age or over are entitled to be registered to vote at local elections for the local electoral area in which they ordinarily live. Citizenship is not a requirement for candidacy or voting at a local election. All members are elected by secret ballot by the system of proportional representation using the single transferable vote. Casual vacancies in membership are filled by co-option (see 3.1). Local authorities annually elect a Cathaoirleach from among their members, who presides at meetings of the council (2.3).

Section 2.2
Term of Office

2.2   Elected members come into office seven days after polling day and hold office for five years, that is until seven days after the polling day at the next local elections – which are by law held in the month of May or June on a day fixed by the Minister for the Environment, Heritage and Local Government. Elected members are expected to attend meetings regularly of the full council and of committees of which they are members, although it may occasionally be the case that members may not be able to fulfil their obligations due, for example, to ill-health. Under the Local Government Act 2001, a member is deemed to have resigned from membership of a local authority if s/he is continuously absent from all council and all relevant committee meetings for a continuous period of six months. However, before the expiry of this period a local authority may by resolution grant an extension for a further six months where the absence is due to illness or occurs in good faith due to other reasons; only one further subsequent such extension may be granted, subject to a maximum period of eighteen months continuous absence. A member may voluntarily resign from membership at any time by notice in writing signed by him or her and delivered to the principal offices of the local authority, thus causing a casual vacancy.

Section 2.3
Cathaoirleach/Mayor

2.3.1   Each local authority must elect one of its members as Cathaoirleach to hold office for a term of one year until a successor is elected at the next annual meeting (a person may be re-elected for a subsequent term). The election takes place at the annual meeting and is the first business to be transacted. The method of election, for which special rules apply, is set out in law (section 37 of the Local Government Act 2001). A Cathaoirleach may resign from that office at any time and may be removed from office by the council subject to special procedures.

2.3.2   The Cathaoirleach presides at meetings of the local authority where s/he may exercise a second or casting vote in the event of an equal division of votes except in the case of the election of Cathaoirleach. S/he is responsible for the effective conduct of business and maintenance of order at meetings (see 2.4). S/he can requisition a special meeting of the council and obtain information from the manager on relevant matters. In the case of county/city councils, the Cathaoirleach chairs the Corporate Policy Group (CPG), which provides a forum to consider policy positions affecting the whole council (see 2.5.4). The Cathaoirleach is paid an annual allowance fixed by the authority. A further aspect of the office of Cathaoirleach is a representational role on behalf of the local authority at civic, public and ceremonial events. A local authority also elects a Leas-Chathaoirleach who acts in place of the Cathaoirleach where the latter is unavailable.

2.3.3   In the cities of Cork and Dublin the title 'Lord Mayor' is used rather than Cathaoirleach, while a 'Mayor' is elected in the other city councils and in borough councils. A Cathaoirleach is elected to the county councils and town councils. However, the Local Government Act 2001 provides flexibility which allows all local authorities by resolution to adopt the title 'Mayor' or to opt for Cathaoirleach if they so choose. A number of counties and towns have adopted the title of Mayor for their chairperson.

Section 2.4
Meetings of the Council

2.4.1   Local authorities conduct much of their business at meetings of the full council. Such meetings are regulated by law (Part 6 and Schedule 10 of the Local Government Act 2001 and associated regulations – S.I. No. 66 of 2002). There are four types of meetings:

- An annual meeting (held May/June)
- Ordinary meetings (usually held at least monthly)
- A budget meeting (usually towards year end)
- A special meeting (held occasionally).

Each local authority must hold an annual meeting which is held in May or June. It is at this meeting that the Mayor/ Cathaoirleach is elected by the members. Following a local election, the first meeting of the local authority is the annual meeting. In the case of a county council it is normally held on the fourteenth day after polling day; in case of city and town councils it is normally held on the tenth day. It is also at this meeting that different elected members are appointed to various committees of the local authority as well as to other organisations (see 3.2).

2.4.2   In practice, most local authorities hold at least one meeting of the full council every month (usually with the exception of August) and these are known as ordinary meetings. A schedule of ordinary meetings is set out in standing orders (see 2.4.6) or determined by resolution of the council. Meetings of the full council are normally held at the principal offices of the local authority.

2.4.3   Each local authority must hold a budget meeting each year within a prescribed period set by the Minister for the Environment, Heritage and Local Government. The budget meeting tends to take place towards the end of the calendar year to deal with the adoption of the next year's budget by the members (see 4.4.4). This was formerly known as the 'estimates meeting'.

2.4.4   In addition to the annual meeting, ordinary meetings and the budget meeting, a special meeting can also be convened to deal with a particular issue. A special meeting may be convened by the Cathaoirleach; by resolution of the full council, or by five elected members of the local authority if, after they have petitioned the Cathaoirleach, s/he refuses to convene the meeting.

2.4.5   Notification of meetings of the full council are sent to each member specifying the time, date, location and agenda for the meeting. Notification will give three clear days notice for the meeting (in the case of a budget meeting at least seven days notice is given). Non-receipt of a notification by any member does not affect the validity of a meeting or of any act or thing done at a meeting. Public notice is also given at the principal offices of the local authority of the place, date and time of a meeting of the full council. In practice, many local authorities also give public notice of council meetings at additional locations, such as in public libraries, newspapers or on their Internet sites.

Standing Orders

2.4.6   The elected council of each local authority will have adopted what are known as 'standing orders', which are basically the rules determining how meetings of the full council (and possibly of its committees) are conducted. Standing orders will usually set out the order in which matters should be dealt with at meetings. While standing orders are a matter for each local authority, with consequent variations between different local authorities, standing orders must provide for:

- A schedule of ordinary meetings
- The commencement, adjournment and termination of meetings
- The revocation or cancelling of resolutions[*]
- Procedures for dealing with urgent business[*]
- Procedures for voting
- Procedures for the suspension of standing orders[*]
- The address for the delivery or sending of notices (by members) to the manager or meetings administrator.

Elected members will be supplied by their own local authorities with copies of their standing orders.

---

[*]Special weighted majorities apply in these cases – see para. 2.4.10.

Quorum

2.4.7 A minimum number of elected members (known as a 'quorum') must be present in order for a meeting to commence and business to be conducted. The quorum for a meeting of a local authority is set out in law as one fourth of the total number of members of the local authority plus one (where one fourth of such total number is not a whole number, the quorum is the next highest whole number plus one). Whenever a meeting is abandoned owing to failure to obtain a quorum, the names of those members present are recorded.

Conduct of Meetings

2.4.8 Meetings of the full council are presided over by the Cathaoirleach/Mayor. In the event that the Mayor is absent, the Deputy Mayor or Leas-Chathaoirleach chairs the meeting. If both are absent the members present choose from among themselves who will preside at the meeting. The person chairing the meeting has a second or casting vote in the event of there being an equal number of votes on a motion. The only instance where this rule does not apply is in the election of the Mayor/Cathaoirleach. A local authority employee known as the 'meetings administrator' is assigned responsibility for procedural matters relating to the notification and organisation of meetings. Many of the duties of meetings administration were before 2001 performed by the 'county secretary' in county councils, and the 'town clerk' or 'assistant town clerk' in other local authorities and this still applies in some cases. The county/city manager may attend local authority meetings and take part in discussions but may not vote. In the case of a town council, the county manager may delegate his/her functions as town manager to an official who would attend meetings and act in place of the manager.

2.4.9 An elected member or group of members may table a 'notice of motion' at meetings – this is essentially a proposal placed before a meeting requesting or directing a certain course of action by the local authority. Standing orders will often specify the number of notices which may be submitted by any member, and the latest date within which it must be submitted if it is to be included on the agenda for the next meeting. Strictly speaking the term 'resolution' is used to describe a 'motion' which has been passed by the council but often these terms may be used interchangeably. In general, the only items that can be discussed at council meetings are those that are specified on the agenda or those that are required to be dealt with by law. However, standing orders may provide for special arrangements in exceptional circumstances to discuss urgent issues that may arise.

2.4.10 A decision of a local authority which is a reserved function (see 4.1), or is a question that has been presented to the council, is determined by a simple majority of the members present and who vote (and not necessarily the majority of members who are present). As noted at 2.4.8, if there is an equal division of votes, the person chairing the meeting has a second or casting vote. However, while most decisions require a simple majority of the members voting, it should be noted that certain decisions are required by law to

While most decisions require a simple majority of the members voting, it should be noted that certain decisions are required by law to have the support of a specified minimum number or proportion of members.

have the support of a specified minimum number or proportion of members. Such decisions would include for example, the passing of a motion to deal with urgent business or a motion under section 140 of the Local Government Act 2001 (see Appendix 1). Each member present at a meeting has a vote unless specifically excluded (for example, if the member has to absent himself/herself due to a conflict of interest – see 3.3.2). In practice various matters at meetings may often be dealt with by way of a general consensus. However, standing orders will set out the circumstances where a roll call vote is required.

2.4.11 The person chairing a meeting may name an individual member if that member is disorderly at a meeting by persistently disregarding the rulings of the chair, or by behaving irregularly, improperly or offensively, or by obstructing the business of the meeting. Where a member is so named, the chair or any member present may move a motion that the member concerned would leave the meeting. If the council agrees, that member must immediately leave the meeting and will not be entitled to speak or to take any further part in that meeting on that day.

2.4.12 Minutes of meetings of the elected council are drawn up by the meetings administrator, as a record of decisions taken at the meeting. Generally, they are not a verbatim account of the proceedings but will include:

- Date, time and place of the meeting
- Names of the members present
- List of the senior employees of the local authority present
- Reference to any report submitted to the members at the meeting

- Where there is a roll call vote, the number and names of members voting for and against the motion and of those abstaining
- Particulars of all resolutions passed
- Other matters considered appropriate.

A copy of the minutes of a meeting is sent or given to each member of the local authority and must generally be submitted for confirmation as an accurate record at the next following meeting.

2.4.13   The public and the media have a statutory right to attend meetings of the council. However, the council can decide (with the support of at least half of the total number of members of the council) to meet 'in committee' – this essentially means in private – where it believes that the absence of the media and public is desirable because of the special nature of a meeting or of an issue to be discussed and where this is not considered to be contrary to the overall public interest. The intention of this provision however is that it be employed only where necessary and not on a regular or routine basis.

Section 2.5
Local Authority Committees

2.5.1   In many areas of local government activity more in-depth discussion can take place at committee level rather than at meetings of the full council. There is a long-standing practice in local government in both Ireland and in other countries of matters being referred to committees of the council for that specific purpose.

Strategic Policy Committees

2.5.2   Following from the *Better Local Government* White Paper, a new and more structured committee system was introduced for county/city councils replacing, in some cases, a plethora of ad hoc committees which had evolved over the years. Under this new system, each county and city council has established a number of policy-focused committees, known as Strategic Policy Committees (SPCs) reflecting the various local authority programmes such as Housing, Environment, Planning and so on. Each member serves on at least one Strategic Policy Committee. Guidelines issued by the Minister and now underpinned by the Local Government Act 2001 set out the arrangements which apply in relation to the establishment of SPCs and these should be consulted for further information. About two thirds of the membership of SPCs is made up of elected members, with the remainder consisting of representatives of 'sectoral interests' – comprising community, business, trade union, farming, development and environmental interests. The SPCs mirror at local level the partnership approach to national economic and social development. The chairperson of each SPC must be an elected member of the council. The chairs are appointed by the full council for a minimum period of three years and the overall spread of SPC chairs must, in accordance with the guidelines, reflect the political representational spread on the full council.

The chairs are appointed by the full council for a minimum period of three years and the overall spread of SPC chairs must, in accordance with the guidelines, reflect the political representational spread on the full council.

2.5.3 The purpose of SPCs is to provide members with the opportunity for an early and more in-depth input into the local authority's policy development process in partnership with local sectoral interests, and 'to consider matters connected with the formulation, development, monitoring, and review of policy' and to advise the authority accordingly. The SPCs thus provide members with the opportunity to develop a greater role in the strategic development of their councils. The final decision however with regard to reserved functions remains with the full council. Each SPC is supported by a director of service. Town councils also have the option of establishing Municipal Policy Committees (MPCs) to consider policy issues and make recommendations to the town council. MPCs must also have a membership comprised of elected members and sectoral interests.

Corporate Policy Group

2.5.4 The chairpersons of each SPC, as well as the Cathaoirleach of the county/city council together make up the Corporate Policy Group (CPG). The county/city manager also participates and supports the work of the CPG. The role of the CPG is a strategic one; it is intended to link and co-ordinate the work of the different SPCs; and to provide a forum where policy positions affecting the whole council can be discussed and agreed for submission to the full council. It can advise and assist the council and propose arrangements for the consideration of policy matters and the organisation of related business. It can thus give increased focus to the policy role of councillors and enhance the democratic overview of council affairs. The CPG must be consulted by the manager in the preparation of both the corporate plan and the draft local authority budget, and its members represent the elected council on the county/city development board.

A diagrammatical outline is shown below.

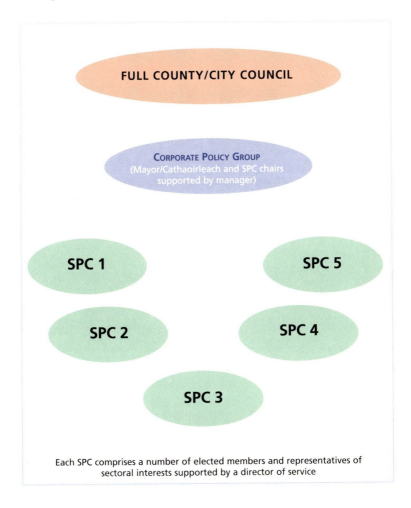

FULL COUNTY/CITY COUNCIL

CORPORATE POLICY GROUP
(Mayor/Cathaoirleach and SPC chairs
supported by manager)

SPC 1

SPC 5

SPC 2

SPC 4

SPC 3

Each SPC comprises a number of elected members and representatives of
sectoral interests supported by a director of service

Area and other Committees

2.5.5 Many county and city councils also conduct business through area committees which deal with issues pertaining to the local area concerned. These are generally based on local electoral areas or a combination of two or more such areas and such committees may meet locally. The Cathaoirleach of a town council that is located within the area of an area committee of a county council is automatically a member of the county council's area committee by virtue of his/her office. A local authority may also establish one or more other (specialist) committee(s) to advise on, or to perform specific functions. Such committees are often of limited duration for a specific task. Also, two or more local authorities may by agreement establish a joint committee to deal with matters of mutual interest to the local authorities concerned. A local authority has discretion to appoint to a committee/joint committee non-councillors with knowledge or experience relevant to its work.

2.5.6 Standing orders (see 2.4.6) adopted by the local authority may include provision in relation to committee meetings, as well as to meetings of the full council. Subject to these and to the terms of the resolution establishing a committee, the committee may adopt its own standing orders. However, the quorum for the meeting of a committee shall not be less than three. While on occasion a committee may meet in private, this is subject to similar requirements as apply for the full council (see 2.4.13). Generally, committee meetings tend to be less formal than meetings of the full council. The law in relation to committees and joint committees is set out in the Local Government Act 2001 (Part 7) and associated regulations (S.I. No. 66 of 2002).

Civic Offices, Waterford County Council

Chapter 3

Elected Members: Practical Issues

Section 3.1
Filling of Casual Vacancies/Co-options

3.1   From time to time, vacancies on a council arise when an elected
       member either dies, resigns or (less frequently) is disqualified
       from membership. Such a vacancy is known as a 'casual
       vacancy', and that member's place is filled by a process known
       as 'co-option'. The co-optee must be nominated[*] by the same
       political party as that for which the outgoing member was
       elected and s/he is then co-opted by resolution to the council as
       a replacement to hold office for the remainder of that member's
       term of office. In cases where a casual vacancy is caused by the
       death or resignation of an independent or non-party member,
       the vacancy is filled according to provisions in the local
       authority's standing orders (see 2.4.6). Where standing orders
       make no provision for such a case the vacancy falls to be filled
       by resolution of the members in the normal way.

Section 3.2
Nominations and Appointments to Other Bodies

3.2.1 A local authority may by resolution nominate a number of its
       members to serve on its own committees and in certain cases on
       the boards of other bodies and organisations. Newly elected
       members should note that this will be one of the main items of
       business to arise for consideration at the first meeting of the

---

[*]There are certain limited exceptions to this requirement, mainly where the
vacancy arises during the local election process.

council after the local elections. At this meeting or subsequently, different members and in some cases non-members with relevant experience will be appointed or nominated to various committees and other organisations, usually for a five-year term. In the case of city and county councils, these bodies are wide-ranging and may include:

* Committees of the local authority itself

* Joint committees between one or more local authorities

* Vocational education committees (VECs, established to oversee vocational education at local level)

* Regional authorities and regional assemblies (see 6.2)

* Regional tourism organisations (established to prepare tourism development plans and promote tourism in different regions)

* Harbour authorities or port companies (established to oversee the operation and maintenance of harbours and ports)

* County/city enterprise boards (established to provide services to assist small companies and promote economic development at local level)

* LEADER groups (established to promote rural development and job creation in local rural areas)

* Area partnership boards (established to support community development initiatives in areas of high unemployment)

* The General Council of County Councils (see 6.4)

* The Association of Municipal Authorities of Ireland (see 6.4)

* The Local Authority Members' Association (see 6.4).

In addition certain other appointments may apply in specific geographic areas – for example certain western counties make appointments to the governing body of National University of Ireland, Galway; local authorities in the greater Dublin area make appointments to the Dublin Transportation Office Advisory Committee and so on. Certain town councils are also involved in making nominations to some of the above bodies. For example, some town councils may make nominations to VECs, and to operational committees of a regional authority, and all town councils holding membership of the AMAI may appoint delegates to that body. There is a general duty for elected members nominated to other bodies to report to the elected council on the activities of that body on an annual basis (or at other times, as requested by the council or Cathaoirleach).

3.2.2   As set out at 2.4.10, while decisions are usually taken by majority vote, special arrangements (known widely as 'the grouping system') are available in relation to the making of appointments to certain committees and other specified bodies. Where two or more appointments fall to be made to such committee or body, such procedures can be invoked by a 'group' of councillors and help provide some element of political proportionality in the appointments process. For further details see Appendix 2. Indeed some local authorities may have by general agreement devised and agreed to operate their own alternative rules designed to achieve a high level of proportionality in the making of appointments.

Section 3.3
Ethics; Declaration of Interests; Codes of Conduct

3.3.1   Part 15 of the Local Government Act 2001 introduced a comprehensive new ethics framework for the local government service, both for elected members and staff. This ethics framework came into operation on 1 January 2003. As a general principle it provides that it is the duty of every member and employee to maintain proper standards of integrity, conduct and concern for the public interest. In addition, it established for each member a system of annual declaration of interests, disclosure of interest in a matter which comes before the authority and a public register of interests. The interests which have to be declared annually are set out in the 2001 Act and associated regulations and include such matters as holdings of land or other property, shareholdings, directorships, contracts with a local authority. Each member must complete and return each year a form setting out his or her interests. Similar arrangements apply to relevant employees.

3.3.2   A member who has actual knowledge that s/he or a connected person* has a pecuniary or other beneficial interest in a matter arising at a council meeting or a committee meeting must disclose that interest, withdraw from the meeting for so long as the matter is discussed and take no part in the discussion or consideration of the matter and cannot vote. Failure to comply with these annual declaration and disclosure requirements is an offence.

3.3.3   A further element of the ethics framework is the Code of Conduct for Councillors. The purpose of this code is to set out

---

*Brother, sister, parent, spouse, partner or child of the person or of the spouse/partner.

standards and principles of conduct and integrity for members, to inform the public of the conduct it is entitled to expect and to uphold public confidence in local government. Each councillor must have regard to and be guided by this code in the exercise of his or her functions and should become familiar with it. A copy of the code of conduct will be supplied to elected members by their own local authorities. A separate code of conduct also applies to employees. These codes supplement and go beyond the specific requirements of the Act.

3.3.4   Under the Local Elections (Disclosure of Donations and Expenditure) Act 1999 as amended, all councillors must make a return of local election expenditure to their local authority within ninety days of polling. Additionally, councillors must make each year a return to the local authority of political donations (if any) received by them. Unsuccessful candidates at a local election must, within ninety days of polling, make a return to the relevant local authority of both election expenditure and a statement of political donations received. Further details and documentation of these requirements is available from the local authority and will be supplied to all members.

Section 3.4
Financial and Other Supports for Elected Members

3.4.1   The ethos of voluntary public service is a long-standing and publicly accepted part of local elected office. Local elected members who run for public office do so knowing that serving as a local authority member involves a substantial commitment of time. However, while not losing sight of this long standing tradition of voluntary civic service, a financial support framework has been introduced in recent years which involves:

- Representational payment (salary type payment)

- Fixed annual allowance (towards meetings and other expenses)

- Ad hoc expenses (conferences and other events)

- Cathaoirleach's allowance

- Allowance for SPC chairperson

- Retirement gratuity – lump sum on retirement.

Additionally certain other bodies to which members are appointed by their local authority may also make allowance payments.

3.4.2   Further information on the local authority financial support framework for elected members is provided in Appendix 3. A local authority is required to maintain a register of payments to councillors.

Information/Training

3.4.3   Elected members may from time to time be authorised by their authority to attend seminars, conferences and training events which are relevant to the work of local government and may receive payments of travel and subsistence expenses for this purpose. Individual local authorities and the different local authority associations may also on occasion organise training/information events. The DEHLG in association with the local government representative bodies also promotes training/information programmes for members. The Local

Government Act 2001 sets out the arrangements for the authorisation of conference attendance. It also requires elected members attending such events to report back and provide a summary of proceedings of such events to the council. Conferences and seminars of relevance to local government can provide useful information to members in carrying out their role and, where attendance is authorised, it is the responsibility of each individual to ensure their full and proper attendance at the events concerned.

Section 3.5
Local Authorities and Oireachtas Members

3.5   Local elected members should be aware that arrangements are also in place to facilitate the relationship between Oireachtas members and local authorities*. A TD or Senator may request to be supplied as a matter of course with local authority documentation such as minutes of meetings of the full council and of specified committees, a copy of the draft development plan etc. They may also attend (but not participate in) local authority meetings. Additionally, a county/city manager is required to make arrangements to meet collectively with local Oireachtas members at least annually.

---

*The Local Government (No. 2) Act 2003 amended the Local Government Act 2001 so that from the 2004 local elections Oireachtas members are disqualified from local authority membership.

Town Hall Theatre, Galway

Chapter 4

Elected Members: Role and Powers

Section 4.1
Policy Role of the Elected Council

4.1.1 As outlined at 1.4, within the local government system major decisions of policy rest with the elected council. The implementation or executive role of day-to-day management rests with a chief executive, the county or city manager. Functions performed by the council are known as reserved functions which are reserved as the exclusive prerogative of the members. The reserved functions of a local authority are performed by the elected members by resolution passed at a meeting of the local authority. They involve decisions on major matters of policy and finance such as:

> *Within the local government system major decisions of policy rest with the elected council.*

– adopting the annual budget

– determining the annual level of commercial rate to be charged

– borrowing money

– making or varying a development plan

– making a special amenity area order

– adopting a scheme of letting priorities for local authority dwellings

– demanding expenses from any other local authority

– making, amending or revoking bye-laws

– bringing enactments into force in the functional area of the local authority

- nominating persons to act on committees or on other public bodies

- nominating a candidate for the Presidency.

A wide range of reserved functions is specified both in the Local Government Act 2001 and across an extensive body of other Acts. A list of the principal reserved functions are set out in Appendix 4 of this booklet.

4.1.2 Some examples may help to illustrate the policy role of the council. Policy in particular areas of the authority's activities is established by the elected council, through for example the development plan, the scheme of letting priorities for local authority dwellings and the annual budget. The manager, in dealing respectively with planning applications, allocation of individual tenancies and authorisation of expenditure must, having regard to any statutory requirements, act in a way that is consistent with the policy which has been established by the members.

4.1.3 While responsibility for performance of local authority functions is shared between the elected members and the manager, the elected local authority members occupy the pre-eminent position of authority and status in the local government system. This derives in particular from the following:

- most of the major decisions of the local authority are reserved as the exclusive prerogative of the elected members, including control over the financial affairs of the authority;

- the policy framework within which the manager exercises executive functions is thus determined by the elected members;

– the elected members enjoy various powers which enable them to oversee and direct the activities of the local authority generally, and ultimately to direct the manager as to the manner in which an executive function is to be exercised in any particular case;

– the fact that the members are directly elected means they have a mandate from the people and an important civic status in relation to the area which they represent.

4.1.4 The division between reserved and executive functions is such that the manager operates within a framework of policy laid down by the elected members. The intention has always been that the members in the exercise of this policy role operate on a basis akin to that of a board of directors served by a full time chief executive. It is the duty of the manager to advise and assist the elected council in respect of the performance by them of their reserved functions. S/he must carry into effect all lawful directions given by the council in relation to the performance of the reserved functions. As provided for in law, the exercise of the policy remit is a fundamental role of the elected council and brings with it a responsibility for necessary preparatory work and proper consideration. Initiatives in recent years such as the improved financial support framework for members, better training/information, the introduction of SPCs and directors of service, are all designed to support councillors in this role. The SPCs in particular are intended to provide councillors with the opportunity for more in-depth involvement in the development, overview and monitoring of policy.

Section 4.2
Representational Role

4.2.1   Local authorities are more than service providers. As democratically elected and accountable bodies they have the authority
and legitimacy to speak and act on behalf of their communities.
The elected council thus acts as a democratic forum for the
representation and articulation of local interests and can
provide civic leadership. It is also by virtue of this mandate that
the members of city and county councils play a significant role
in the election of Seanad Éireann.

4.2.2   The Local Government Act 2001 expressly recognises the
representational role of local elected members. Under the Act,
this role can include communicating the views of the elected
council to other public bodies on the operation of their services
as they affect the local population; carrying out research or
studies into local issues or needs and promoting interest in
democracy and participation in local government on the part of
young people and the public in general. Local authorities also
have a right of representation on a range of other public
agencies that operate locally (see 1.2.3). In addition, local
government's wider role in representing the local community
beyond statutory local authority services is recognised in its
representation on and key role as regards the county and city
development boards (CDBs) (see 6.1).

Section 4.3
General Powers of Members

4.3.1   The powers of local authority members derive primarily from
their reserved functions by way of which the policy of the local

authority is determined. In addition, however, the elected members have various powers under the Local Government Act 2001 in relation to the functions of the manager. These enable the members to play a significant part in overseeing and directing the affairs of the authority generally. The elected members have power to:

- require the manager to attend a meeting of a local authority or a committee of a local authority (s. 152)

- require the manager to inform the members before performing any specified executive function (other than in respect of staff), in a particular instance or generally (s. 138)

- require the manager to submit plans, specifications and cost estimates of particular works (s. 137)

- require the submission of statements of the financial position of the authority (s. 105)

- prohibit the undertaking of new works subject to certain exceptions (s. 139) (similar powers apply in certain circumstances under the Planning and Development Act 2000 (s. 179))

- oversee proposals for land disposal (s. 183)

- require the manager to obtain a second legal opinion as regards the exercise of a reserved function (s.132)

- require that a particular act, matter or thing be done by the manager (s. 140: see Appendix 1).

4.3.2   Additionally, the Cathaoirleach or the elected council can obtain information from the manager on any business or transaction of the authority   (s. 136). Managers' orders, which set out executive decisions, must also be available for inspection and a copy of a manager's order must be made available to a member on request (s. 151). The elected members also enjoy extensive powers in relation to the local authority budget and the overview of financial affairs generally, as set out at 4.4.

Section 4.4
Local Authority Budget and Financial Affairs

4.4.1 An outline of the general system of local authority financing is set out at 1.3. As already indicated, spending by local authorities is divided into current (sometimes called revenue) expenditure and capital expenditure, which form separate accounts. The local authority budget is based on current expenditure which covers the day-to-day running of the local authority (including staff salaries; housing maintenance; operational costs of treatment plants etc). The adoption of the annual budget is a key function of the elected council.

4.4.2 As part of the local authority budgetary process, each year a draft budget must be drawn up in a particular format showing proposed expenditure levels for the various local authority services for the forthcoming year. The draft budget is broken down across the eight service programme groups (housing, roads etc. – see table at 1.2). Each programme group is in turn further broken down into programmes. The draft budget will show the estimated income and expenditure for each programme and programme group. Some services are provided by county councils in town council areas (e.g. library, fire services, register of electors) and the town council contributes to the cost by way of a payment to the county council which appears in the town draft budget as a 'county charge'. In the preparation of the draft budget for a county/city council the manager must consult with the corporate policy group who in

Budget Preparation Process

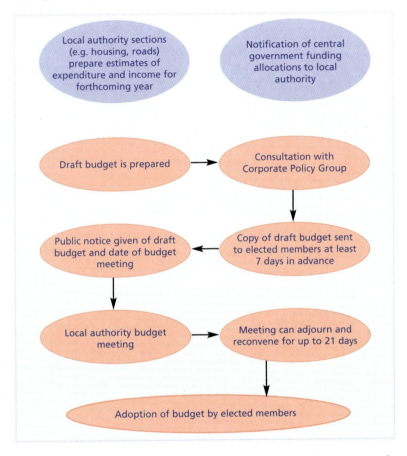

the process may avail of relevant expertise. A diagrammatic outline of the budget preparation process is set out at 4.4.3.

4.4.3   Local authorities are required by law to adopt a budget that is sufficient to meet their proposed expenditure – total estimated expenditure must be met by the total estimated income from commercial rates, charges for goods and services, and grants.

As well as adopting the budget for the coming year, the elected members of a rating authority* must also determine the annual rate on valuation (formerly known as 'the rate in the pound') to be levied on commercial properties. The budget for those town councils who are not rating authorities is financed mainly by way of an addition to the county rate in the town.

Budget Meeting

4.4.4   The draft budget is considered at a meeting of the council known as the 'local authority budget meeting' which must be fixed for a date which is within a period (usually towards the end of the year) prescribed by regulations. When the draft budget has been prepared, and at least seven days before the day on which the budget meeting is to begin, a copy of the draft budget must be supplied to each member of the local authority. A copy must also be available for public inspection at the offices of the local authority and be supplied on request to any interested member of the public (at a nominal charge). The elected council is not bound to adopt the draft budget as submitted and may revise and amend it if it thinks it necessary, subject to it being sufficient to enable the local authority to carry out its functions. The budget meeting itself may be adjourned from time to time by the members (and reconvened) to allow for further consideration of the issues. However at the budget meeting itself, or at any later adjournment(s) of the meeting held within the following twenty-one days, the budget must be adopted, with or without amendment as the council may decide. Ultimately, failure to comply with the statutory duty to adopt an adequate budget can lead to removal of the council from office. The annual rate on valuation and certain

---

*The rating authorities comprise county/councils, borough councils and certain town councils.

charges for goods and services are also determined at the budget meeting as a direct consequence of the expenditure levels provided for in the budget which is adopted.

Additional Expenditure

4.4.5　The budget as adopted by the council fixes the current income and expenditure of a local authority for the year in question. The manager cannot exceed the total expenditure provided in the budget for any particular purpose save with the authorisation by resolution of the elected members. The council may, if it so wishes, adopt a scheme permitting the manager to incur additional expenditure without authorisation in circumstances specified by them but subject to remaining within the overall budget level. In exceptional circumstances only (emergencies or receipt of additional funding at short notice) can the manager incur additional expenditure beyond that provided for in the budget; and in this situation the Cathaoirleach must be informed and the matter brought to attention of the members at the next practicable meeting of the authority.

Annual Financial Statement

4.4.6　An annual financial statement (AFS) together with a report by the manager (including details of over budget expenditure) must each year be sent to the elected members and considered at a meeting of the authority, subject to a minimum of seven days notice. The AFS shows details of actual income and expenditure incurred for the previous year under the various programme groups, compared directly with the amounts provided for in the budget for that year. Subsequently, when the AFS has been audited, it must again be submitted to the elected council along with the local government auditor's report (see 4.4.13).

Financial Statements and Reports to Council

4.4.7 Apart from the annual budget and the AFS there are other powers which allow for financial overview. The elected council or the CPG may, by resolution, require the submission of such financial statements by the manager setting out the financial position of the local authority as they may decide. Such statements must contain any details and be supplied at any intervals as are specified by the council (s. 105). Also, the elected council may at any time by resolution require the manager to prepare plans, specifications and costings for any works (s. 137). Additionally, the manager must as a matter of course and without a resolution inform the elected council before undertaking any new works (other than works of maintenance or repair or certain urgent works) and before committing the authority to expenditure in connection with them (s. 138(1)).

Borrowing, Lending and Financial Assistance

4.4.8 The borrowing of money by a local authority, subject to the sanction of the appropriate Minister (normally the Minister for the Environment, Heritage and Local Government), or the lending of money to another local authority, is a reserved function.

4.4.9 The grant of financial assistance under the broad powers conferred on local authorities to promote community interest is a reserved function (including assistance to local groups for amenity, recreational, community and other purposes).

Community Fund/Community Initiative Scheme

4.4.10 The elected council may, by resolution, establish a separate 'community fund' to support specific community initiatives such as amenity, recreational, environmental or community development projects of benefit to the area concerned. Contributions to the community fund may be made by local voluntary, business or community groups, and may be raised by the local authority by way of a community initiative scheme. It is a matter for the elected members to decide whether to adopt a community initiative scheme, following a process of local consultation. Such a scheme is based on the payment of an annual contribution by each household for a specified number of years towards a particular community initiative of benefit to the local community. Details of the project, the amount of the annual contribution, waiver arrangements, the period for which it is operable and the area to which it applies must be set out in the scheme (sections 109, 110).

Capital Expenditure

4.4.11 The manager is required to submit each year to the elected council a report on the proposed programme of capital projects for the following three years, which can be considered at the budget meeting or such other meeting as may be decided by the elected members (s. 135). This report usually takes the form of a multi-annual capital programme for the various local authority services (e.g. roads, sanitary etc).

As already set out at 1.3.2, capital expenditure is funded by State grants; local authority internal capital receipts (sale of property; development levies) and local authority borrowing.

Such borrowing must be approved by the elected council and both a scheme of development levies and proposals for property disposal must come before the council for consideration. The manager is required to bring proposals for new works to the attention of the members. Usually they will come before the council in accordance with the planning code or other statutory approval procedures for specific projects. More generally, elected members are required to consider the longer-term development needs and consequent capital requirements of their area at various times such as, for example, when assessing along with the manager the housing needs in the preparation and review of the housing strategy and when making the local authority development plan, the scheme of development levies, the water quality plan, the library development programme and other such longer-term plans.

Local Government Audit

4.4.12 The audit of local authority accounts, both current and capital, is carried out by local government auditors, who are independent in the performance of their functions and are under the general control of a director of audit. Local authority staff and elected members have a statutory duty to co-operate with them. An auditor may disallow illegal or unfounded payments, surcharge such payments on the persons responsible whether on members or the manager, and charge on the person the amount of any loss or deficiency incurred through misconduct or negligence (see also 5.3.13).

4.4.13 Following receipt by the local authority of the audited AFS and any auditor's report, the manager must submit both for consideration by the elected council which may establish an audit committee to consider the matter and report back to them.

Financial Management System (FMS)

4.4.14   The roll out to local authorities of a new and modern financial management system called Agresso was completed in 2003. This new system is based on up-to-date and best accounting principles and replaced the outdated cash-based system of accounting in local authorities. The new financial management system provides better management information, facilitating maximisation of financial efficiency, accountability and value for money. In addition, the creation of new posts of finance/management accountants, who work directly to heads of finance, is intended to strengthen the financial management framework in local authorities.

Carndonagh Environmental Improvement Scheme, Donegal

Local Authorities: Manager and Staff

Section 5.1
County/City Manager

5.1.1 Each county and city council has a chief executive, who is known as either the county manager or city manager and who is an employee of that authority. As well as being the manager for the county council, a county manager is also manager for every town council or borough council within the county. Where certain joint bodies (e.g. joint library committee) operate in two or more counties or in a city and one or more counties, the Minister for the Environment, Heritage and Local Government determines which of the managers concerned shall be manager for those joint bodies.

5.1.2 The position of county/city manager is filled following a competitive recruitment process organised by an independent central agency, The Local Appointments Commission (LAC)*. The manager is appointed by the elected council on the recommendation of the Commission for a contract term of seven years, although this may be extended by three years. Subject to special procedures a manager can be suspended, or removed from employment by a county council or city council with the consent of the Minister.

Deputy Manager

5.1.3 A manager may, after consultation with the Cathaoirleach of the county or city council, appoint a deputy manager to act as

---

*The LAC is due to be restructured under the Public Service Management (Recruitment and Appointment) Bill 2003.

manager during periods of leave or other absence of the manager; or if circumstances require and such appointment has not been made, it may be made by the Cathaoirleach. Where the post of manager becomes vacant the Local Government Act 2001 requires the Minister to appoint a person to be the manager temporarily. The temporary appointment continues until a permanent appointment is made, but it may be terminated at any time.

Delegation of Functions

5.1.4   In reality, it is not possible for any one individual to carry into effect all executive functions and, consequently, it is normal practice to delegate some functions to directors of service and other staff. The elected council must be notified of such delegation. However the manager continues to be responsible for the acts of the delegate and can either revoke a delegation or directly perform any particular function which has been delegated. As chief executive, the manager retains the ultimate responsibility for ensuring the efficient and effective overall operation of the local authority and the carrying into effect of the policy decisions of the elected council.

Section 5.2
Local Authority Staff

5.2.1   The manager is ultimately responsible for staffing and organisational arrangements in the local authority for which s/he is manager. In recent years a more structured management tier was introduced which resulted in the appointment of directors of service in county and city councils. The directors are given responsibility for the delivery of specified services (e.g. housing) and related functions are usually delegated by the manager. A key element of the role of a director of service in county and city councils is also to support the relevant Strategic Policy Committee (SPC) in carrying out its work (see 2.5.2).

5.2.2   County and city councils, and many town councils, employ a variety of staff to carry out the different services provided by local authorities. As regards local authority meetings, all local aurhorities are served by a meetings administrator ('town clerk' in town councils) and other officials. Staff are appointed either on a full-time or a contract basis and carry out specific duties. Local authorities across the country currently employ over 33,000 people, who work across the full range of local government services. These can vary from administrative staff who may be charged with carrying out a range of duties within service areas, such as housing, planning, library, the fire service or roads, to professional and technical staff in different fields (e.g. engineers, planners, architects, conservation officers, librarians, fire officers, laboratory technicians, financial accountants, IT specialists, vets). Staff employed by county councils are often assigned to town councils from a unified staff structure serving both town and county. In practice, a county manager may designate an official, usually a director of service, to act as 'town manager' and carry out the duties of manager with respect to a specific town council.

5.2.3   A spirit of cooperation and mutual understanding between elected members and local authority staff is important for the effective discharge of local authority business. The following excerpt from the Code of Conduct for Councillors (see 3.3.3)

summarises the situation well:

> Both councillors and staff have the common interest of serving the community. But their responsibilities are distinct. Councillors are responsible to their electorate for their elected term of office. Staff are responsible to the manager in carrying out their duties. Mutual respect and courtesy between councillors and employees is essential to good local government and should be maintained at all times.

Section 5.3
Functions of Manager

Executive Functions

5.3.1   As noted at 4.1, while the main policy-making decisions are reserved to the elected members (these are known as 'reserved functions'), the manager carries out what are known as 'executive functions'; these are defined in law as all functions which are not designated as reserved functions. Executive functions include decisions in relation to staffing matters, recovery of debts, court actions, acceptance of tenders, collecting rates and rents, making lettings for local authority dwellings, determination of planning applications and taking enforcement action. These are decided by the manager and/or nominees of the manager. In practice, many day-to-day executive functions are delegated by the manager to directors of service and other officials. The Local Government Act 2001 provides that the manager perform executive functions in accordance with the policy framework established by the elected members – members establish this policy framework through the exercise of reserved functions which set out plans and overall strategies (e.g. library development programme; scheme of housing letting priorites). The manager carries out executive functions by means of what are known as 'manager's orders' – written, signed and dated orders setting out decisions made (see 5.3.9).

5.3.2   The fact that executive functions are undertaken by the manager is intended to facilitate the prompt and efficient discharge of on-going local authority business, and allow members the time to focus on policy matters with the support of an experienced full-time chief executive. In practice, the effective discharge of local authority business is dependent on both the elected members and the manager working together for the common good. Various provisions of the Local Government Act 2001 provide for the supply of information by the manager to the elected members and allow them to maintain an overview of local authority affairs generally. The duties of the manager in this regard include those set out below.

Attendance of Manager at Meetings

5.3.3   A manager has the right to attend meetings of a local authority and to take part in discussions as if a member, but without the right to vote. Insofar as is consistent with the due performance of duties, the manager must attend any meeting of a local authority or committee of a local authority whenever requested to do so by that authority. The manager must, when attending a meeting, give the local authority or committee all advice and assistance which can reasonably be required and must, for that purpose, arrange for the attendance at the meeting of such other officials of the authority as may be appropriate.

Furnishing of Information/Reports

5.3.4   The Act empowers a council as a whole or the Cathaoirleach to obtain all information in the possession or procurement of the manager on any business or transaction of the authority (section 136).

5.3.5   Under the Act, the elected members may at any time, by resolution, require the manager to inform them of proposals before performing any specified executive function (other than in respect of staff) of the local authority. The resolution may apply to any particular instance or to every instance of the performance of the specified function (section 138).

5.3.6   Under the Act, the elected members may, by resolution, require the manager to submit to them plans and specifications for any particular work which can lawfully be executed by the local authority, together with an estimate of the cost of the work (section 137).

5.3.7   The corporate policy group (CPG) (see 2.5.4) may request a report from the manager on any matter related to a function of the authority, which the manager must provide. In such circumstances the Cathaoirleach may direct the manager to refrain for a limited period from performing a specified executive function (section 133(5)).

5.3.8   The elected members may direct the manager to obtain a second legal opinion in respect of the exercise of a reserved function (section 132(2)).

Managers' Orders

5.3.9 Under the Act, any member of a local authority is entitled, on demand, to be supplied with a copy of any specified order made by the county/city manager. A manager must also keep a register containing a copy of every order, available for inspection. Orders made by a deputy manager, or by a director of service or other employee under a delegation, are subject to the same requirements. The manager must inform the elected members of the appointment of a deputy manager and of the delegation of functions (section 151).

Financial Statements and Reports

5.3.10 The manager must provide financial information to the council as part of the budget process, the AFS and additionally as may be requested at any time by the elected council or CPG. See 4.4.4 to 4.4.13 for further information.

Information and Direction on New Works

5.3.11 The manager must, as a matter of course and without a resolution, inform the members before undertaking any new works (other than works of maintenance or repair or works arising from emergencies or certain other urgent and necessary works to provide accommodation) and before committing the local authority to any expenditure in connection with them. The local authority members may, subject to certain exceptions, prohibit the undertaking of works, provided they are not works which the local authority is required by law to undertake.

Requisition by Elected Members

5.3.12   The manager must comply with any valid resolution passed by the members under section 140 of the 2001 Act as to the manner in which an executive function is to be exercised in any particular case (see Appendix 1).

Obligation on Manager in relation to Proposals by Members

5.3.13   Whenever a proposal is made at a meeting of a local authority to do anything which is a reserved function, or is a matter which is covered by a resolution under section 140 of the 2001 Act, and in consequence of which an illegal payment is to be made, or a deficiency or loss is likely to result in the funds of the local authority, the manager (or any employee nominated by the manager) is required to object and to state the grounds of the objection. If a decision is taken on the proposal, the names of the members voting for, voting against and abstaining from voting are recorded in the minutes. The members who vote for the proposal are alone liable in the event of any charge or surcharge being made by an auditor as a result of the decision (see also 4.4.12).

Chapter 6

Local Government: The Wider Context

The Local Dimension: County and City Development Boards

6.1.1   A county/city development board (CDB) operates under the aegis of each county or city council. The boards bring together all players locally – the public sector agencies, the social partners, local government and local development – to seek common cause in developing their counties and cities, to plan for the future with better co-operation and co-ordination and to operate in a more integrated way. CDBs thus offer an opportunity for local authorities to influence the way various public bodies deliver services in their area. Members of the board are drawn from the following four sectors.

> *County and City Development Boards bring together all players locally – public sector agencies, the social partners, local government and local development – to seek common cause in developing their counties and cities, to plan for the future with better co-operation and co-ordination and to operate in a more integrated way.*

- local government: county or city councillors (the Cathaoirleach of the council and the chairs of the council's strategic policy committees), the county/city manager and a town councillor

- social partners: representatives drawn from the business and employers, agriculture and farming, trade union, and community and voluntary sectors

- representatives from the State agencies operating locally, e.g. health boards, regional offices of the Department of Education and Science, VECs, Gardaí, Enterprise Ireland, FÁS, Teagasc, IDA Ireland, regional tourism organisations, Údarás na Gaeltachta

- local development: representatives from the county/city enterprise board, area partnership companies, ADM-supported community groups and LEADER groups.

6.1.2   The chair of the CDB is a local authority member and the board is supported by a director of community and enterprise, a senior local authority official. During 2001-2002, each CDB drew up a ten year strategy for the economic, social and cultural development of its area, involving extensive consultation. The strategy is designed to act as a template for the provision of public services in each county and city area. Also, as part of their remit, CDBs have responsibility for the endorsement of plans prepared by relevant community and local development agencies.

Section 6.2
The Regional Dimension: Regional Authorities and Regional Assemblies

6.2.1   Ireland has eight regional authorities, established in 1994. The membership of the regional authorities comprises county/city councillors appointed by each of the constituent local authorities from among their members. The regional authorities have a dual role, to promote the co-ordination of public services at regional level and to monitor and advise on the implementation of EU Structural Fund spending in their area. They are also responsible for the preparation of regional planning guidelines under the National Spatial Strategy.

6.2.2   There are, in addition, two regional assemblies which were established in 1999. The two assemblies (the Border, Midland and Western Regional Assembly – known as BMW – and the Southern and Eastern Regional Assembly) are the managing authorities for the Regional Operational Programmes in their regions under the 2000-2006 National Development Plan. They also monitor the general impact of all EU programmes under the NDP/Community Support Framework in their areas and promote co-ordination of the provision of public services in their regions. The membership of the regional assemblies is drawn from the membership of the constituent county and city councils.

6.2.3   Details of the composition of regional authorities and regional assemblies are set out in Appendix 5.

Section 6.3
The National Dimension: Government Departments

6.3.1   One of the roles of national government in Ireland, as in other countries, is to provide the framework within which local government operates. This is done through the enactment of legislation by the Oireachtas, by way of regulations, and issue of policy guidelines, consultation papers etc. by Ministers; and via circular letter from government departments to local authorities. National government also makes an important contribution to local government finances. There is regular communication, both formal and informal, between local government and central government departments.

6.3.2   National policy responsibility for local government lies with the Department of the Environment, Heritage and Local Government (DEHLG) which is the main focus of contacts between national and local government. Such contacts include regular communication with the local government associations at elected and official level; information and training seminars; working groups; visits to local authorities by Ministers and meetings with local elected members and officials.

6.3.3   Local authorities also interact with various other government departments on a range of issues which impact on their operations. Examples are set out in the table on page 65.

Section 6.4
The National Dimension: Local Government Associations

6.4.1   There are three national local government associations, which represent the collective interest of local government and members. The General Council of County Councils (GCCC), originally founded in 1899, represents the interests of county and city councils, all of which are members and each of which appoints three delegates to the GCCC. The Association of Municipal Authorities of Ireland (AMAI), established in 1912, is the equivalent association representing the town councils and city councils. Both associations are funded by contributions from their respective constituent local authorities and nominate members to the Congress of Local and Regional

Government Department	Local government related responsibilities
Agriculture and Food	diseases of animals, veterinary, abattoirs
Arts, Sport and Tourism	arts, sports, swimming pools, regional tourism organisations
Communications, Marine and Natural Resources	regional fisheries boards, harbours, coastal protection, forestry
Community, Rural and Gaeltacht Affairs	local development, LEADER, area partnerships, drugs task forces, community development support programmes, Gaeltacht, Islands
Defence	Civil Defence
Education and Science	VECs, higher education grants
Enterprise, Trade and Employment	County enterprise boards, casual trading
Environment, Heritage and Local Government	local government system (including finance, personnel, non-national roads, planning policy, water services, housing, fire services, library, environmental services)
Finance	EU monitoring committee, arterial drainage and flood relief (OPW), valuation for rating (Valuation Office)
Health and Children	health and child related services including Comhairle na nÓg
Justice, Equality and Law Reform	coroners, pounds, courthouses, childcare, liquor licensing
Social and Family Affairs	supplementary welfare, school meals
Transport	national roads (National Roads Authority) and road safety

Authorities of Europe (see 6.7). A third association, the Local Authority Members' Association (LAMA) was founded in 1980 to represent the specific interests of elected members.

6.4.2   The representative associations organise regular meetings, conferences and seminars for elected members on topical local government issues and participate in a training programme for councillors promoted by Department of the Environment, Heritage and Local Government. The associations also provide information services to elected members. Through the feedback received from elected members at these fora, policy submissions are made by the associations to national government. In addition, regular meetings are held between the associations and the DEHLG. In this way, the associations act as a channel of communication and consultation on local government matters between elected members, Ministers and their Departments. The AMAI and GCCC are also nominating bodies to the administrative panel for elections to the Seanad, and have the right to nominate members of certain boards.

6.4.3   The associations are formally recognised by the Local Government Act 2001. Under the terms of the Act their role includes

* undertaking research and other studies
* promoting education and training
* providing policy support and other assistance to the constituent local authorities on local government issues
* making submissions to the Minister or other public authorities.

The Act requires that the associations operate in accordance with a constitution, proper financial and accounting procedures and adopt an annual report.

Section.6.5

The National Dimension: Local Government Commission

6.5   Part 11 of the Local Government Act 2001 will on commencement provide for the establishment of an independent Local Government Commission. The Commission would meet as required to make recommendations to the Minister concerning:

- proposed changes to local authority boundaries
- changes to local electoral areas and the number of seats assigned to each
- proposed changes to the number of elected members of a local authority
- proposal for establishment or dissolution of a town council
- other local government matters referred by the Minister.

Section 6.6

The European Dimension: EU Committee of the Regions

6.6.1   Increasingly local government has been affected by policy initiatives originating from the European Union. This has manifested itself not only in EU funding for local authority projects but also in legislation and regulatory requirements which affect the operation of various local government services (e.g. water quality, public procurement, waste disposal etc).

6.6.2 The EU's Committee of the Regions (CoR) represents local and regional government in the EU policy formation and decision-making processes. The committee, which is an advisory body consulted by the other EU institutions in respect of various policy areas, is composed of 317 members from all twenty-five member states. Of these, there are nine Irish members and nine alternates. The Irish members, all of whom are county or city councillors, are proposed by the Minister for the Environment, Heritage and Local Government, nominated by the Government and formally appointed by the EU Council of Ministers. The selection process must have regard to the objective that the Irish delegation as a whole should reflect appropriate geographic and gender balance and have a broad political spread. Support for the delegation is provided through a secretariat attached to the Dublin Regional Authority.

Section 6.7
The European Dimension: Council of Europe's Congress of Local and Regional Authorities of Europe

6.7 The Congress of Local and Regional Authorities of Europe (CLRAE) is a consultative body within the framework of the Council of Europe (an entirely separate organisation to the EU). It has a membership of forty-five countries and focuses in particular on human rights, democracy and the rule of law. The Council publishes reports, studies and recommendations on local government. The Congress' main objective is to support and promote local democracy and it has assisted in the establishment of local and regional democratic structures in central and eastern Europe. It promotes the implementation of the European Charter of Local Self-Government which is an international convention to safeguard local democracy; the Charter was ratified by Ireland in 2002. Ireland has four members on the CLRAE – the GCCC and the AMAI nominate two members each. Secretariat support is provided by the GCCC. The CLRAE membership comprises 313 members drawn from all forty-five member states.

Appendix 1

Requisition to Manager

Section 140 of the Local Government Act 2001 (which replaced section 4 of the City and County Management (Amendment) Act 1955) provides that the members of a local authority may by resolution require the manager to do any particular act, matter or thing which can lawfully be done. The manager is then obliged to comply with the resolution if, and to the extent that, money for the purpose has been provided. A resolution under section 140 may not, however, extend to any function in relation to staff. Nor may it be framed in such terms so as to bind the manager to a particular course of action on every occasion where the exercise of the relevant function may be involved or so as to prevent the performance of a function which is required by law or by order of a court to be carried out.

The notice of intention to propose a resolution under section 140 must be signed by three members and at least seven days notice of the intention to propose the resolution must be given to the manager, who must send a copy of the notice to every member of the local authority. The resolution may be considered at an ordinary meeting or at a specially convened meeting for the purpose. The motion to pass the resolution must be dealt with before any other business of the meeting (other than the election of a Cathaoirleach) but the elected council has discretion to take other business first if it decides that such other business should take precedence. A simple majority of the members present and voting is sufficient to enforce the requisition, providing that the number voting exceeds one-third of the total membership of the local authority.

Special provisions apply, under section 34(7) of the Planning and Development Act 2000, to the proposing and passing of resolutions under section 140 relating to decisions on planning applications and certain other matters. If all the land in question is located in a single local electoral area, the notice of intention to propose the resolution must be signed by three quarters of the members of the local authority from that area. If the land is situated in more than one local electoral area, the notice of intention must be signed by three quarters of the members from each of the areas concerned. It is necessary for the passing of such a resolution under section 140 that not less than three quarters of the total membership of the local authority vote in its favour.

There is a special procedure for cases in which a manager receives notice of intention to propose a resolution under section 140 which, if passed, would require the manager to decide to grant planning permission for development which, in his or her opinion, would contravene materially the development plan. In such a case, the manager must within seven days of receiving the notice, make an order invoking the procedure set out in section 34(6) of the Planning and Development Act 2000. Where such an order is made, the Act provides that the notice of intention to propose the section 140 resolution has no further effect. The manager must then publish notice of the intention to consider deciding to grant the permission and give a copy of this notice to the applicant and any person who has objected in writing to the proposed development. The planning authority must duly consider any objection or representation received within four weeks of the first publication of the notice and may then pass a resolution requiring that a decision to grant permission be made by the manager. Under section 34(6) it is necessary for the passing of such a resolution that not less than three quarters of the total membership of the planning authority vote for it.

In certain limited circumstances the operation of section 140 is restricted by law, e.g. under waste management legislation.

Appendix 2

Appointments to Committees and Certain Other Bodies – Grouping System

1. The Local Government Act 2001 (Paragraph 18 of Schedule 10) allows for a 'grouping system' to operate in relation to the making of two or more appointments by a local authority to its own committees, joint committees or joint boards. Under the Act this system also applies to appointments by a local authority to the following: VEC; harbour authority; regional authority/assembly; regional tourism organisation; GCCC; AMAI; county enterprise board; LEADER Group; DTO advisory committee; area partnership board.

2. Under the system it is open to any 'group' of members to obtain an appointment. The number necessary to form a group is calculated by dividing the number of members present at the meeting at the time when the business of making the appointments to the particular body or committee is reached by the number of appointments to be made. Where the number so obtained consists of a whole number and a remainder the next highest whole number applies. A person nominated by a group automatically stands appointed on such nomination and without a vote. For example twenty-two members are present in the chamber when the business of making appointments to the body concerned is reached and five appointments are to be made; any five persons can therefore form a group and nominate a person, who is then appointed on such nomination without a vote. A person may not be a member of more than one group in relation to the appointment of members to a particular committee/body.

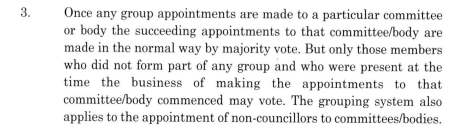

3.   Once any group appointments are made to a particular committee or body the succeeding appointments to that committee/body are made in the normal way by majority vote. But only those members who did not form part of any group and who were present at the time the business of making the appointments to that committee/body commenced may vote. The grouping system also applies to the appointment of non-councillors to committees/bodies.

4.   While the operation of the grouping system is optional, it remains as a right for any group wishing to operate those procedures and cannot be removed or interfered with in any way. The forming of groups is however discretionary. Members do not have to form groups. Indeed some local authorities have in the past by way of general agreement among the members devised their own rules to promote fairness and equity across the totality of appointments to be made by the authority. A high degree of proportionality across the various interests represented on the council is thus achieved. Paragraph 19(2) makes clear that a local authority is free to devise such local arrangements.

5.   Similar provisions to the grouping system apply to port companies by virtue of regulations made under the Harbours Act 1996 (S.I. No. 335 of 1996 and 34 of 2002).

6.   Where by law special knowledge or experience is required in relation to a particular appointment, such a requirement continues to apply. Equally where an appointment is made by virtue of a particular office (e.g. Mayor/Cathaoirleach) it is not affected by the grouping system.

7.   Special arrangements apply in relation to appointments to SPCs. Under the Act such appointments must be made in accordance with guidelines issued by the Minister and the spread of SPC chairs should reflect the spread of interests represented on the council. See 2.5.2 of this booklet.

Appendix 3

Financial Support Framework for Members

1.   **Introduction** – The main elements of the financial support framework for elected members are outlined below. This is a summary and not a full statement of the detailed rules and regulations relating to each scheme. A local authority is required to maintain a public register of such payments. It is open to a member to decline payment under any scheme. All amounts shown below are those applying as at January 2004.

2.   **Representational Payment (RP)** – This salary type payment was introduced with effect from 1 January 2002. The RP is linked to a Senator's basic salary and increases are automatically applied to the RP on a pro-rata basis. It is subject to PAYE in the normal way and to the appropriate rate of PRSI. Only one RP applies to a person who is a member of more than one local authority. In the event of continuous absence from all meetings (council and relevant committees) the full RP is paid for the first six months. If that absence is approved and continues, half the RP will apply for the second six months. Thereafter it terminates. It should be noted however that, apart from the RP, under the Local Government Act 2001 continuous absence leads to a termination of membership – see 2.2 of this booklet. The current rates of RP are shown in Table 1.

3   **Annual Allowance** – All councillors receive a fixed annual allowance designed to defray in a structured way reasonable expenses incurred by them in attending meetings associated with their council business.

3.2   For members of city and county councils, the annual allowance is calculated using a formula based on: (i) distance* from an

* For 0-10 miles, a ten-mile distance applies.

Table I: Rates of RP from 1/1/2004		€
Local Authority		
A	County/City Councils	14,137 pa
B	Borough Councils and Athlone, Bray, Dundalk, Ennis and Tralee Town Councils	7,070 pa
C	Arklow, Athy, Balbriggan, Ballina, Ballinasloe, Birr, Buncrana, Bundoran, Carlow, Carrickmacross, Carrick-on-Suir, Cashel, Castlebar, Castleblayney, Cavan, Clonakilty, Clones, Cobh, Droichead Nua, Dungarvan, Enniscorthy, Fermoy, Greystones, Kells, Killarney, Kilrush, Kinsale, Leixlip, Letterkenny, Listowel, Longford, Macroom, Mallow, Midleton, Monaghan, Mullingar, Naas, Navan, Nenagh, New Ross, Portlaoise, Shannon, Skibbereen, Templemore, Thurles, Tipperary, Trim, Tullamore, Westport, Wicklow and Youghal Town Councils	3,533 pa
D	Remaining Town Councils	1,928 pa

individual's home to the council HQ; (ii) a mileage rate (max. rate); (iii) a subsistence rate (seven hours plus); (iv) an index of either 30, 50, 70 or 80, reflecting a notional number of meetings for the different groupings of local authorities (see details at 3.4 of this appendix), and supplemented for those groupings by (v) a fixed amount for general representational expenses (€2,285.53; €2,412.50; €2,539.48 or €2,666.45 per annum). The formula used to determine the annual allowance is set out in Table II, followed by a working example for a city/county councillor in the 30 Index group living 27 miles from council HQ.

3.3   A margin of tolerance of up to 20% non-attendance is allowed. In other words a member who attends at least 80% of the council/ committee meetings which s/he was due to attend in a year will qualify for the full travel and subsistence element of

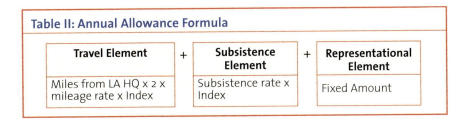

Table II: Annual Allowance Formula

Travel Element	+	Subsistence Element	+	Representational Element
Miles from LA HQ x 2 x mileage rate x Index		Subsistence rate x Index		Fixed Amount

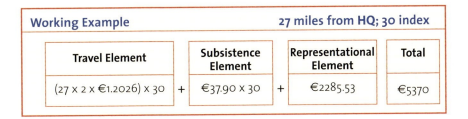

Working Example　　　　　　　　　　　　**27 miles from HQ; 30 index**

Travel Element		Subsistence Element		Representational Element	Total
(27 x 2 x €1.2026) x 30	+	€37.90 x 30	+	€2285.53	€5370

the annual allowance and will qualify for the full representational element if s/he attends at least 50% of those meetings. Reduced annual allowances apply in cases where these attendance thresholds are not reached.

3.4　　The applicable index in accordance with the above formula is as follows: **30-index group:** Carlow, Cavan, Kilkenny, Laois, Leitrim, Louth, Longford, Monaghan, North Tipperary, Offaly, Roscommon, Sligo, South Tipperary, Waterford and Westmeath County Councils; Galway and Waterford City Councils. **50-index group:** Clare, Donegal, Galway, Kerry, Kildare, Limerick, Mayo, Meath, Wicklow and Wexford County Councils; Cork and Limerick City Councils. **70-index group:** Dun Laoghaire-Rathdown, Fingal and South Dublin County Councils. **80-index group:** Cork County Council and Dublin City Council.

3.5 Members of borough and town councils receive a lump-sum annual allowance of €2,736; €1,729 or €864 in line with categories B, C and D in Table I on page 76. A member of a borough or town council who attends at least 80% of the council/ committee meetings which s/he was due to attend will qualify for full payment of the first three quarters of the above allowance, with a 50% attendance requirement for receipt of full payment of the remaining quarter. Reduced annual allowances apply in cases where these attendance thresholds are not reached.

4. **Ad-hoc expenses** – In addition to the annual allowance, members may receive ad hoc travel and subsistence payments in respect of attendance at conferences, training courses, meetings in relation to twinning matters or participation in delegations to Ministers etc. outside of the home city/county. Payments may also be received in respect of authorised foreign travel. These payments are subject to the prior authorisation of the council; members must submit a summary of the proceedings of the meeting or event attended to the next meeting of the council. In cases of travel by car, the current (2004) mileage rates are shown in Table III.

Table III: Mileage Rates			
Ad hoc mileage a calendar year	Engine capacity up to 1200cc	Engine capacity 1201cc to 1500cc	Engine capacity 1501cc and over
	cent	cent	cent
Up to 4,000	86.05	101.27	120.26
4,001 and over	43.50	50.29	56.40

The current (2004) subsistence rates are shown in Table IV.

Table IV: Subsistence Rates		
Night Allowance	**Day Allowance**	
	Absence of seven hours or more	Absence of three hours or or more but less than seven hours
€133.72	€37.90	€15.45

5.   **Retirement Gratuity** – This involves a lump sum calculated as 3/20 of RP (on retirement) for each year of service since May 2000, up to a maximum twenty years service, and with a minimum three-year service requirement. Subject to certain conditions, the gratuity is payable on a councillor's retirement whether voluntarily, or due to failure to be elected, death or ill health.

6.   **Strategic Policy Committees (SPCs) Chairs' Allowance** – An allowance of up to €5,079 per annum may be paid to councillors who chair Strategic Policy Committees (SPCs) in a city/county council. The decision to pay an allowance and its amount, subject to a maximum of €5,079 pa, is a matter for determination by the members of the local authority.

7.1   **Other Allowances** – Local authorities may pay an annual allowance to the Cathaoirleach for the reasonable expenses of that office. A decision to pay an allowance and the determination of the amount is a matter for decision by the elected council. In practice the amount paid varies to reflect the demands of the office in different authorities. The taxation implications of these payments have been determined by the Revenue Commissioners – 50% of the allowance, subject to a fixed minimum amount of €5,000 and a maximum of €10,000, may be paid without deduction of tax, with PAYE/PRSI deducted on the balance. Any allowance for the Leas-Chathaoirleach must reflect the limited statutory role of the position, a modest sum approximate to likely expenses.

7.2   **Other Bodies** – Certain other bodies to which councillors are appointed (e.g. regional authorities/assemblies) also make allowance payments to their members. Such payments are a matter for the organisations concerned.

8.   **Further information** – All queries in relation to any of the above matters should be directed to the member's own local authority or, in the case of other bodies, to the body concerned. Queries in relation to taxation should be directed to the member's own local tax office.

Appendix 4

Reserved Functions
Financial Matters and General Corporate Affairs

- adopting the local authority budget and determining the annual rate on valuation (section 103 of Local Government Act 2001)
- adopting a demand to meet the expenses of certain town councils or joint body (section 103 of Local Government Act 2001)
- borrowing money or lending of money to another local authority (section 106 of Local Government Act 2001)
- decisions relating to charges for certain services provided by a local authority (Local Government (Financial Provisions) (No. 2) Act 1983)
- establishing a community fund to support community initiatives (section 109 of Local Government Act 2001)
- adopting a scheme for the making of an annual contribution by households towards a specified community initiative(s) (section 110 of Local Government Act 2001)
- authorising the incurring of additional expenditure and adopting a scheme for that purpose (section 104 of Local Government Act 2001)
- requiring the preparation and submission to the council of financial statements (section 105 of Local Government Act 2001)
- requiring a manager to submit plans, specifications and an estimate of costs of any particular works specified in the resolution (section 137 of Local Government Act 2001)
- deciding on when a report on the capital programme is to be considered, if not at the budget meeting (section 135 of Local Government Act 2001)
- entering into an agreement with another local or public authority for the discharge by one of the local authorities concerned of the functions of the other local or public authority (section 85 of Local Government Act 2001)

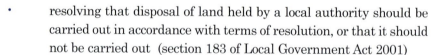

- resolving that disposal of land held by a local authority should be carried out in accordance with terms of resolution, or that it should not be carried out (section 183 of Local Government Act 2001)
- adopting the annual report (section 221 of Local Government Act 2001)
- approving the corporate plan with or without amendment (section 134 of Local Government Act 2001)
- deciding to confer a civic honour on a person (section 74 of Local Government Act 2001)
- deciding to enter into twinning arrangements (section 75 of Local Government Act 2001)
- deciding to incur reasonable expenditure for receptions/ entertainment expenses (section 76 of Local Government Act 2001)
- nominating a person to be a candidate at an election for the office of President of Ireland (section 16 of Presidential Elections Act 1993)
- appointing, whether by way of nomination or election, of a person to be a member of a public authority (schedule 14 to Local Government Act 2001)
- making or revoking of an order or the passing or rescinding of a resolution by virtue of which an enactment is brought into operation in or is made to apply to the functional area or a part of such area of a local authority, the application to be made to any Minister in respect of the making or revoking of any such order (schedule 14 to Local Government Act 2001)
- making of boundary alteration proposal, making statement of response, amending boundary proposal following statement of response, deciding to apply for boundary alteration, town requesting own county to apply for boundary alteration into another county and consideration of such request (sections 29 and 30 of Local Government Act 1991 and S.I. No. 37 of 1993)[†]
- adopting a proposal to alter the number of members of certain local authorities (section 22 of Local Government Act 2001)[†]

- decisions in relation to a proposal for the establishment of a new town council (section 185 of Local Government Act 2001)[†]
- directing a manager to inform the council of the manner in which s/he proposes to perform any specified executive function (section 138 of Local Government Act 2001)
- directing that works should not proceed (section 139 of Local Government Act 2001)
- requiring a manager to do or effect a particular act specifically mentioned in a resolution which the manager or local authority concerned can lawfully do or effect etc (section 140 of Local Government Act 2001)
- resolving to extend a direction to a manager under section 133 of Local Government Act 2001 to refrain from doing a particular act
- directing that a second legal opinion be obtained regarding the exercise and performance of a reserved function (section 132 of Local Government Act 2001)
- electing a Cathaoirleach or a Leas-Chathaoirleach of a local authority by that authority or of a chairperson of a joint body (schedule 14 to Local Government Act 2001)
- deciding to pay and determination of amount of reasonable allowance for Cathaoirleach or Leas-Chathaoirleach (section 143 of Local Government Act 2001)
- deciding to pay certain expenses to non-members of a local authority for attendance at committees and deciding to pay and determination of amount of SPC chair allowance (Local Government (Expenses of Local Authority Members) Regulations 1993, S.I. No. 391 of 1993)
- adopting or reverting to the title 'Cathaoirleach' and 'Leas-Chathaoirleach' or the title 'Mayor' and 'Deputy Mayor' (section 32 of and schedule 8 to Local Government Act 2001)
- the removal of the Cathaoirleach or Leas-Chathaoirleach from office (section 34 of Local Government Act 2001)

- appointing or removal of a manager by a county council or city council (sections 145 and 146 of Local Government Act 2001)
- extending the period of permitted absence for councillors (section 18 of Local Government Act 2001)
- establishing a committee to advise the authority on matters connected with its functions; the delegation of certain functions to committees and appointment of members (councillors and non-councillors) to a committee (Part 7 of Local Government Act 2001)
- establishing a joint committee of 2 or more local authorities to consider and advise on specified matters; the delegation of certain functions and appointment of members (councillors and non-councillors) to a joint committee (section 52 of Local Government Act 2001)
- requesting a report from councillors regarding the activities of bodies to which they are appointed by the local authority (section 141 of Local Government Act 2001)
- authorising representation by councillors at seminars, conferences, etc (section 142 of Local Government Act 2001)
- deciding to hold or to cease to hold membership of an association of local authorities (section 225 of Local Government Act 2001)
- deciding to meet 'in committee' for whole or part of a meeting because of the special nature of an item of business or for other special reasons and where it is considered such action is not contrary to the overall public interest (section 45 of Local Government Act 2001)
- making of rules under section 127 of Local Government Act 2001 as to arrangements for the attendance and raising of issues by interested persons at meetings of the authority or of its committees
- procedure at any meeting of a local authority or joint body (schedule 14 to Local Government Act 2001)

- making, amending or revoking standing orders; deciding on days and times of meetings and fixing regular schedule of meetings by resolution or by standing orders; deciding to hold a special meeting; making additional arrangements for giving public notice of meetings; making rules for ensuring the fair and equitable appointment of members to other bodies (schedule 10 to Local Government Act 2001)
- making a scheme for waiver of rates and determination of classes of relevant property for which rates may be payable by instalments (sections 2 and 4 of Local Government (Rates) Act 1970)
- the demanding (however expressed) under any enactment of the whole or a part of the expenses of a local authority or of a joint body from any other local authority (schedule 14 to Local Government Act 2001)
- approving the transfer of functions of joint burial board to local authority (section 230 of Local Government Act 2001)†

Housing

- adopting a tenant purchase scheme (section 90 of the Housing Act 1966 as substituted by section 26 of the Housing (Miscellaneous Provisions) Act 1992)
- making an agreement between authorities to enable an authority to perform its housing functions outside its functional area (section 109 of Housing Act 1966)
- adopting a report on housing requirements (section 8 of Housing Act 1988)
- adopting or amending a scheme of priorities for letting dwellings or making a determination to set aside dwellings for certain categories of housing need (section 11 of Housing Act 1988)
- entering into agreement between a county council and certain town councils that the county council will be responsible for management of some or all of town council's houses (section 20 of Housing Act 1988)

- adopting or amending a statement of policy to counteract undue social segregation in housing (section 20(1A) of Housing Act 1988 as inserted by section 28 of Housing (Miscellaneous Provisions) Act 1992)
- determining terms and conditions under which a housing authority may provide assistance to other housing authorities and approved bodies (section 6 of Housing (Miscellaneous Provisions) Act 1992)
- adopting a statement of policy regarding management of the housing stock (section 9 of Housing (Miscellaneous Provisions) Act 1992 and section 58 of Housing Act 1966)
- transferring, selling or assignment of mortgages, unless it is the subject of a direction by the Minister (section 14 of Housing (Miscellaneous Provisions) Act 1992)
- adopting a Traveller accommodation programme or amending or replacing such a programme and making of an appointment to a local Traveller consultative committee (sections 7, 14 and 22 of Housing (Traveller Accommodation) Act 1998)
- making and amending a scheme of allocation priorities for affordable houses sold under Part V of Planning and Development Act 2000 (section 98 of Planning and Development Act 2000)
- making and amending a scheme of allocation priorities for affordable houses sold under the 1999 affordable housing scheme (section 8 of Housing (Miscellaneous Provisions) Act 2002)

Roads and Road Traffic

- making representations to the Garda Commissioner and the Minister for Transport in relation to certain proposed bye-laws to be made by the Commissioner under the Road Traffic Acts (section 6 of Road Traffic Act 1961)$^\Sigma$
- making of arrangements in relation to school wardens (section 96 of Road Traffic Act 1961 and S.I. No 37 of 1993)

- entering into agency agreement with another authority to carry out functions re traffic wardens (section 7 of Local Authorities (Traffic Wardens) Act 1975 and S.I. No. 37 of 1993)
- making an agreement with Waterways Ireland to transfer responsibility for a canal bridge to a road authority (section 16 of Canals Act 1986)
- declaring a public road and consideration of objections or representations (section 11 of Roads Act 1993 as amended by section 180 of the Planning and Development Act 2000)
- abandoning a public road and consideration of objections or representations etc (section 12 of Roads Act 1993)
- making representations to NRA regarding proposed alignment of a national road in certain circumstances (section 22 of Roads Act 1993)
- making or revoking a toll scheme in relation to a regional or local road and the making of representations to the NRA on a toll scheme relating to a national road (sections 57 and 60 of Roads Act 1993 as amended by sections 271 and 273 of Planning and Development Act 2000)
- making of toll bye-laws in relation to a regional or local road (section 61 of Roads Act 1993 as amended by section 274 of Planning and Development Act 2000)
- entering into an agreement for financing, maintenance, construction and operation of toll roads on a regional or local road (section 63 of Roads Act 1993 as amended by section 275 of Planning and Development Act 2000)
- making of bye-laws to regulate and control skips on public roads and consideration of objections or representations (section 72 of Roads Act 1993)
- making of an order to provide for the extinguishment of a public right of way and the consideration of objections or representations etc (section 73 of Roads Act 1993)

- functions of a road authority re abandonment of railway line (section 21 of Transport Act 1950)
- making of speed limit bye-laws and the making of representations by town councils in relation to such bye-laws (section 46 of Road Traffic Act 1961 as substituted by section 33 of Road Traffic Act 1994)
- specifying the places in which vehicles may be parked either indefinitely or for any period not exceeding a specified period subject to regulations to be made by Minister* (section 35 of Road Traffic Act 1994)
- making of bye-laws for the control and regulation of the parking of vehicles in specified places on public roads including payment of parking fees and the consideration of observations or representations in relation to the draft bye-laws and the making of a resolution to indicate the manner in which parking fees shall be disposed of (section 36 of Road Traffic Act 1994)
- deciding to provide a 'special category sign' in accordance with regulations to be made by Minister*(section 95 of Road Traffic Act 1961 as amended by section 37 of Road Traffic Act 1994)
- deciding to provide or remove certain classes of traffic calming measures to be prescribed by the Minister* and the consideration of observations or representations in relation to such proposals (section 38 of Road Traffic Act 1994)
- declaring or extending or altering of a taximeter area and the determination of maximum fares for hire of taxis and wheelchair accessible taxis (Road Traffic (Public Service Vehicles) (Amendment) Regulations 1995 S.I. No. 136 of 1995 as amended by Road Traffic (Public Services Vehicles) (Amendment) (No. 3) Regulations 2000 S.I. No. 367 of 2000)°
- making of bye-laws in relation to stands for taxis (section 15 of the Road Traffic Act 2002)

Planning and Development

- making of a development plan and making etc. of a variation of a plan in force (sections 9, 11, 12 and 13 of Planning and Development Act 2000)

- deciding to make or amend etc. a local area plan (section 20 of Planning and Development Act 2000 as amended by section 9 of Planning and Development (Amendment) Act 2002)

- requiring the granting of permission for the development of land which would contravene materially the development plan (section 34 of Planning and Development Act 2000)

- revoking or modifying a planning permission to develop land (section 44 of Planning and Development Act 2000)

- decisions in relation to a development contribution scheme (section 48 of Planning and Development Act 2000)

- amending a supplementary development contribution scheme (section 49 of Planning and Development Act 2000)

- adding to or deleting from record of protected structures (section 54 of Planning and Development Act 2000)

- approval etc of a special planning control scheme (sections 85 and 86 of Planning and Development Act 2000)

- making, subject to variations and modifications, or deciding not to make a draft planning scheme (section 169 of Planning and Development Act 2000)

- amending or revoking a planning scheme (section 171 of Planning and Development Act 2000)

- deciding to vary, modify or not to proceed with proposals regarding local authority own development (section 179 of Planning and Development Act 2000)

- making of a special amenity area order (section 202 of Planning and Development Act 2000)

- making etc of a landscape conservation area order (section 204 of Planning and Development Act 2000)

- making etc a tree preservation order (section 205 of Planning and Development Act 2000)
- making etc an order for the creation of a public right of way (section 207 of Planning and Development Act 2000)
- varying, modifying or deciding not to proceed with a proposal for the holding of an event by a local authority (section 238 of Planning and Development Act 2000)
- making etc of an agreement between two or more planning authorities for sharing the cost of performing functions under Act (section 244 of Planning and Development Act 2000)
- deciding the manner in which weekly list of planning applications shall be made available to councillors (article 27 of Planning and Development Regulations 2001, S.I. No. 600 of 2001)
- deciding the manner in which weekly list of planning decisions shall be made available to councillors (article 32 of Planning and Development Regulations 2001, S.I. No. 600 of 2001)

Environmental Services and Protection

- formulating a proposal to take a supply of water from a source of water (section 2 of Water Supplies Act 1942)
- examining and considering a drainage scheme sent to a county council by the Commissioners of Public Works and providing observations on the scheme to the Commissioners (section 5 of Arterial Drainage Act 1945)
- considering reports on coast erosion, and declaring that the promotion of a coast protection scheme is expedient; considering reports of the Commissioners of Public Works on the feasibility of preparing and executing a coast protection scheme, and declaring whether or not such a scheme would be prepared and executed; making a declaration whether or not a coast protection scheme is to be proceeded with or revoking such a declaration (sections 2, 5, 8 and 10 of Coast Protection Act 1963)

- making of contribution towards person engaging in water pollution research (section 29 of Local Government (Water Pollution) Act 1977 and S.I. No. 37 of 1993)
- making of an agreement by a fire authority to provide services for or avail of the services of any body or person other than a fire authority and the making of agreements between fire authorities (section 10 of Fire Services Act 1981)
- making and revision of fire and emergency operations plans (section 26 of Fire Services Act 1981)
- making of submissions to a fire authority regarding a proposed indoor event that requires a licence (section 23 of Licensing of Indoor Events Act 2003)
- making of a financial contribution by a local authority for research, surveys, investigation or educational programmes relating to air pollution (section 18 of Air Pollution Act 1987)
- making etc of a special control area in order to prevent or limit air pollution (section 39 of Air Pollution Act 1987)
- making etc of an air quality management plan (section 46 of Air Pollution Act 1987 as amended by section 102 of Environmental Protection Agency Act 1992)
- entering into an agreement with the Environmental Protection Agency to carry out a function or service on behalf of the Agency (section 45 of Environmental Protection Agency Act 1992)
- making etc of a litter management plan (section 13 of Litter Pollution Act 1997)
- establishing a programme of measures in relation to a river basin district (article 12 of European Communities (Water Policy) Regulations 2003, S.I. No. 722 of 2003)
- making and updating of a river basin management plan (article 13 of European Communities (Water Policy) Regulations 2003, S.I. No. 722 of 2003)

- approving a draft bye-law, consideration of submissions in relation to draft bye-laws and the making, amending, revoking of bye-laws under general powers contained in section 37 of Local Government Act 1994 relating to (i) use, operation, protection of land, facilities etc under control of the local authority or (ii) to regulate, control a specified activity or nuisance[†] (this is a general power to make bye-laws, other Acts may confer specific bye-law making power in relation to a particular issue)

- making of bye-laws prohibiting or regulating specified agricultural, horticultural or forestry activities responsible for water pollution (section 21 of the Local Government (Water Pollution) (Amendment) Act 1990 and S.I. No. 78 of 1999)

- making of bye-laws specifying the manner in which waste is presented for collection (section 35 of Waste Management Act 1996 and section 52 of Protection of Environment Act 2003)

- making of bye-laws for purposes of preventing the creation of and controlling litter (section 21 of Litter Pollution Act 1997 as substituted by section 57 of the Protection of the Environment Act 2003)

- making of bye-laws re control/regulation etc of casual trading; extinguishment of a market right owned by a local authority (sections 6 and 8 of Casual Trading Act 1995)

- making of bye-laws declaring areas to be control areas where horses must be licensed (sections 13 and 17 of Control of Horses Act 1996)

- making etc of bye-laws relating to control of dogs (section 17 of Control of Dogs Act 1986 as amended by Control of Dogs (Amendment) Act 1992)[†]

- making of bye-laws in relation to the use of and safety of navigation within harbours under control and management of local authority and the imposition of charges (section 89 of Harbours Act 1996)

- making, amending or revoking of a bye-law by a local authority under any other enactment where the provisions governing such making, amendment or revocation do not provide that it is a reserved function (schedule 14 to Local Government Act 2001)
- entering into or terminating an arrangement with another local authority in relation to application for and granting of horse licences (section 20 of Control of Horses Act 1996)
- giving of consent to certain exemptions re licensing of horses (section 19 of Control of Horses Act 1996)
- adopting a resolution regarding special late closing hours of licensed premises in the whole or part of the local authority's administrative area; the District Court shall have regard to the terms of such resolution (section 11 of Intoxicating Liquor Act 2003)

Recreation, Amenity and Community Matters

- making or revoking an order prohibiting the erection or retention of temporary dwellings (section 31 of Local Government (Sanitary Services) Act 1948 and S.I. No. 45 of 1948)
- making of bye-laws in respect of the use of temporary dwellings (section 30 of Local Government (Sanitary Services) Act 1948)[†]
- making of bye-laws in respect of swimming baths and swimming places etc (sections 41 and 42 of Local Government (Sanitary Services) Act 1948) [†]
- making bye-laws in respect of national monuments owned by local authority (section 9 of National Monuments (Amendment) Act 1987)
- representing the views of a local community (section 64 of Local Government Act 2001)
- deciding to provide assistance in money or in kind to promote the interests of a local community (section 66 of Local Government Act 2001)

- adopting a library development programme (section 78 of Local Government Act 2001)
- declaring that a body is a recognised association for the purposes of promoting the interests of the local community (section 128 of Local Government Act 2001)

Miscellaneous

- adopting list of qualified electors and changing name of street or locality; adopting list of qualified electors and applying to Government for an order changing name of an urban district, town, townland or non-municipal town and consent by county council (sections 76 to 79 of Local Government Act 1946, as amended by section 53 of the Local Government Act 1955 and section 67 of the Local Government Act 1994)[†]
- adopting or rescinding Part III of Gaming and Lotteries Act 1956 which permits the licensing for gaming of amusement halls and funfairs (section 13 of Gaming and Lotteries Act 1956)
- preparing and submitting higher education grant schemes to the Minister for Education and Science and submitting amendments to such schemes (section 5 of Local Authorities (Higher Education Grants) Act 1968)
- arranging for performance of suitable local authority functions by a health board (section 25 of Health Act 1970)
- applying a school meals scheme to a school which lies outside the authority's functional area, providing meals other than to national schools by city councils (sections 274 and 279 of Social Welfare (Consolidation) Act 1981 and S.I. No. 37 of 1993)
- entering into arrangements for the execution of dog control functions including the granting of assistance (section 15 of Control of Dogs Act 1986 as amended by section 6 of Control of Dogs (Amendment) Act 1992 and S.I. No. 37 of 1993)
- making of decision to provide public abattoir (section 19 of Abattoirs Act 1988 and S.I. No. 37 of 1993)

- making a polling scheme (section 28 of Electoral Act 1992 as amended by section 2 of Electoral (Amendment) Act 1996)
- issuing of polling information cards, where regulations provide, by a local authority (section 27 of Local Government Act 2001)

Explanatory Notes

❒ Chapter 4 gives a general outline of the powers vested in the elected council. These are known as reserved functions and are exercised by resolution passed at a meeting of the local authority. An outline of the main reserved functions is set out in this Appendix but these may not vest to the same degree in all types of local authority: reference should be made to the particular Act or regulation.

❒ In a number of cases special statutory requirements/procedures may apply in relation to the exercise of a function by the elected council (e.g. election of Cathaoirleach; grouping system and appointments to committees; motions under section 140 of Local Government Act 2001); or the law may provide for circumstances where if a reserved function is not exercised that function may fall to be carried out by the executive.

❒ For presentation reasons the categorisation of functions in this Appendix does not follow exactly that used in the programme groups for local authority budgetary purposes.

---

† Provisions in Local Government Act 2001 to apply on commencement.
Σ Provisions in Road Traffic Act 2002 to apply on commencement.
* Minister for Transport
° Provisions in Taxi Regulation Act 2003 to apply on commencement.

Appendix 5

Regional Authorities and Regional Assemblies

Regional authority	Constituent city/county councils
Border	Cavan, Donegal, Leitrim, Louth, Monaghan and Sligo
Dublin	Dublin City, Dún Laoghaire-Rathdown, Fingal and South Dublin
Mid-East	Kildare, Meath and Wicklow
Midlands	Laois, Longford, Offaly and Westmeath
Mid-West	Clare, Limerick City, Limerick County and North Tipperary
South-East	Carlow, Kilkenny, South Tipperary, Waterford City, Waterford County and Wexford
South-West	Cork City, Cork County and Kerry
West	Galway City, Galway County, Mayo and Roscommon
Regional assembly	**Constituent city/county councils**
Border, Midland and Western (BMW)	Cavan, Donegal, Galway City, Galway County, Laois, Leitrim, Longford, Louth, Mayo, Monaghan, Offaly, Roscommon, Sligo and Westmeath
Southern and Eastern (S&E)	Carlow, Clare, Cork City, Cork County, Dublin City, Dún Laoghaire-Rathdown, Fingal, Kerry, Kildare, Kilkenny, Limerick City, Limerick County, Meath, North Tipperary, South Dublin, South Tipperary, Waterford City, Waterford County, Wexford and Wicklow

Appendix 6

Acronyms of Relevance to Local Government

ABP   An Bord Pleanála – www.pleanala.ie
ADM   Area Development Management – www.adm.ie
AFS   Annual Financial Statement
AMAI   Association of Municipal Authorities of Ireland –
           www.amai.ie
BLG   *Better Local Government* (1996 White Paper)
BMW   Border, Midland and Western Regional Assembly
           – www.bmwassembly.ie
CCMA   County and City Managers' Association
CEB   County Enterprise Board
CLRAE   Congress of Local and Regional Authorities of
           Europe – www.coe.int/t/e/CLRAE
COMHAR   National Sustainable Development Partnership –
           www.comhar-nsdp.ie
COR   Committee of the Regions – www.cor.eu.int
CDB   County/ City Development Board – www.cdb.ie
CPG   Corporate Policy Group
DEHLG   Department of the Environment, Heritage and
           Local Government - www.environ.ie
ENFO   Environment Information Service – www.enfo.ie
EPA   Environment Protection Agency – www.epa.ie
EU   European Union – www.europa.eu.int
FMS   Financial Management System
GCCC   General Council of County Councils –
           www.councillors.ie
HFA   Housing Finance Agency – www.hfa.ie
HSA   Health and Safety Authority – www.hsa.ie
IEI   Institute of Engineers of Ireland – www.iei.ie
IMPACT   Irish Municipal Public and Civil Trade Union –
           www.impact.ie
IPA   Institute of Public Administration – www.ipa.ie

IPI	Irish Planning Institute – www.irishplanninginstitute.ie
IT	Information Technology
LAC	Local Appointments Commission – www.publicjobs.gov.ie
LAFMS	Local Authority Financial Management System
LAMA	Local Authority Members' Association – www.lama.ie
LEA	Local Electoral Area
LGCSB	Local Government Computer Services Board – www.lgcsb.ie
LGF	Local Government Fund
LGMSB	Local Government Management Services Board – www.lgmsb.ie
MPC	Municipal Policy Committee
NBA	National Building Agency – www.nba.ie
NGO	Non-Governmental Organisation
NILGA	Northern Ireland Local Government Association – www.nilga.org
NRA	National Roads Authority – www.nra.ie
PCP	Public Capital Programme
PPP	Public Private Partnership – www.ppp.gov.ie
RP	Representational Payment
RTPI	Royal Town and Planning Institute – http://ireland.rtpi.org.uk
SEO	Senior Executive Officer
SIPTU	Services Industrial Professional and Technical Union – www.siptu.ie
S&E	Southern and Eastern Regional Assembly – www.seregassembly.ie
SMI	Strategic Management Initiative – www.bettergov.ie
SPC	Strategic Policy Committee
VEC	Vocational Education Committee
VFM	Value for Money

Index

Index

Index